IT BEGAN WITH A DREAM

IT BEGAN WITH A DREAM

DR. GLADYS B. WEST

with M. H. JACKSON

IGWEST

King George, Virginia

IGWEST
It Began With A Dream

Published in the United States by IGWEST Publishing, King George, Virginia.
Available at Amazon. Also available at Amazon as an eBook on Kindle.

Photograph credits: Interior photos courtesy the West family archive, the Virginia
State University Archives, the U.S. Navy, and the U.S. Air Force.
Cover Design: Andre Jones
Cover Photography: Andre Jones
Copy Editing: Erica Young, Joyful Editing

Written by: Dr. Gladys B. West with M. H. Jackson
For information contact us on Facebook, Instagram, and Twitter @drgladysbwest

LCCN – 2020906510
ISBN: 978-0-578-67638-8 (paperback)
ISBN: 978-0-578-67639-5 (e-book)

The manuscript is based on the life story as told by Dr. Gladys B. West.
Information regarding the history of the Naval Surface Warfare Center at
Dahlgren is from Naval Sea Systems Command History at navsea.navy.mil.

To my parents, Nolan and Macy Pearl Brown, whose strong shoulders I stood on to dream. To my loyal and dedicated husband, who continues to stand by my side after 63 years of marriage. To my children, grand-children, brothers, sisters, nieces, and nephews, who encouraged and supported my effort to let others hear my dreams.

———————————

To the strong women in my life who said I could do it. Thank you!

CONTENTS

FOREWORD

Every time you use your cell phone map function to get directions, you can thank Dr. Gladys West. And with the estimates, there are more than 5 billion people worldwide that have mobile phones; that's a lot of "thank you's." How often do we ask ourselves how did we ever manage without GPS on our phones and in the same breath exclaim how grateful we are for their accuracy? How many knew Dr. West, a woman petite in stature, though enormous in brilliance, would positively impact daily lives?

I was honored to meet Dr. West when invited to attend her induction into the United States Air Force Space and Missile Pioneers Hall of Fame, one of the Air Force Space Command's highest honors. As she accepted the honor, the twinkle in her eyes was reflective of her literal knowledge of our earth and space. Her humble presence was reflective of a woman who was not only a pioneer of our GPS technology but also a woman so pleased she had her family and friends surrounding her during this momentous occasion. To put it in perspective, our Air Force has over 650,000 uniformed and civilian Airmen. And that day, in the hallowed halls of the Pentagon, many of us assembled to honor Dr. Gladys West for her contribution to our Air Force, our Nation, our world. And although Dr. West's civilian career was with the Navy, the Global Positioning System (a constellation of orbiting satellites) is operated and controlled by the U.S. Air Force. Her work exemplified the Air Force's core values: integrity first, service before self, and excellence in all we do. Dr. West shared that she had no idea, at the time, that her work would affect so many: "When you're working every day, you're not thinking, 'What impact is this going to have on the world?' You're thinking, 'I've got to get this right.'" That's integrity, service, and excellence rolled into one.

Over 40 years prior, when I was graduating college and entering the Air Force to serve first as an engineer and then on to pilot training, Dr. West was a civilian working for the Navy, and her data ultimately became the basis for the Global Positioning System (GPS). Her work was already influencing my career as we use GPS to navigate the skies as aviators.

My parents were born just a few years after Dr. West and only one hour south of her hometown of Sutherland, VA. Their upbringings were humble, and when my father entered the Air Force, it allowed my parents to leave the South and live in and explore the world. I was fortunate to enjoy that worldly exposure that Dr. West always dreamed of.

From the humblest beginnings, Dr. West, a phenomenal woman, shares her story with such grace, dignity, and passion; it inspires all of us regardless of race, gender, or age. Because of her outstanding achievements, women of color don't have to walk the same impoverished path she did; they can forge new paths of their own, fully acknowledging we have figuratively "big shoes to fill."

Dr. West's life story empowers all women, especially women of color, to realize we are no longer "hidden figures." There are no boundaries to what we can accomplish on earth or in space, and our contributions are greatly needed in all aspects of STEM (Science, Technology, Engineering, and Math). The solutions to our world's greatest challenges are within us! It is imperative that we find our passions, learn, and persist to achieve our goals.

Thank you, Dr. West, for paving the way.

Lt. General Stayce D. Harris, USAF (Retired)

IT BEGAN WITH A DREAM

INTRODUCTION

I will forever remember growing up on that small farm in Dinwiddie County, Virginia. I recall crossing the railroad tracks and walking three miles to the segregated Butterwood Road School. It was the stereotypical little one-room schoolhouse, with rusty, decrepit furniture, sometimes leaky ceilings, and always hand-me-down books. All the "Colored" children in the area, from first through seventh grade, crowded into one room, with one overworked and grossly underpaid teacher. The black teachers were paid only about one-half of their white counterparts' salaries. The white folks called it separate but equal, but there was nothing equal about it. Every day I wished and dreamed of having more – more books, more classrooms, more teachers, and more time to dream and imagine what life would be like if only I could fly away from the strenuous and seemingly never-ending work on our family farm. I just had to get away from that farm someday. It surely was not the place for an open-minded girl like me, with big city dreams. I continued to dream beyond my wildest imagination, and no matter how inconceivable those dreams, I still had hope for a better life ahead. All these years later and I have never found myself living in a big city. Still, my journey has been an amazing one, with some unbelievable, big city things happening quite regularly along the way.

My most incredible and exciting moment in all these years came after I decided to go back to school later in life with another degree in mind. I was at an age where most of my peers were already retired or at least thinking about it. Just as well, I had accomplished a lot more than most women by this stage of my life, but I still felt something was missing. I was always committed to be the best, and to be my absolute best, I just had to go for it. The letters "Ph.D." would look quite nice at the end of my name, now wouldn't it? If I could earn that degree, I would finally feel like I went all the way. As my husband, Ira, would say, "it would be like hitting a home run and then touching all the bases in baseball." Maybe then I would be satisfied.

Despite having thirty-nine years of experience as a mathematician for the United States Government, I still had an insatiable thirst for knowledge. I always had this sense that there was more to accomplish. Even when I was a little "colored" girl growing up in rural Virginia in the 1930s attending that segregated school with worn and outdated books, I always dreamed of being more and achieving more. When I reflect on my years living with and working for Dr. John Hunter and his wife, Dr. E. Louise Hunter, a "power couple" at my alma mater, Virginia State, before the term power couple was thought of, I now realize how much of a positive influence they had on me while I was an undergraduate student. Their example alone was enough to inspire me to go as far as I could as a scholar, and their advice and guidance were priceless.

I had discovered at an early age that education could open many doors in life and enable me to see what the world was like outside of the rural countryside of Dinwiddie County. I made a commitment to be the best I could be and absorb as much knowledge that a little farm girl could handle. So now, when I should have been thinking about retiring and sitting in my sunroom with my feet up, the only question regarding the Ph.D. was, "Do I still have it in me to do it?" Because by this time, I was no spring chicken if you know what I mean.

My husband had already retired after 35 years of civilian service with the Navy, and my daughter Carolyn was grown with a school-age son. As it happens, there were many challenges that I faced along the way to earning that doctorate degree, but I met them with gusto, which was the only way I knew how. I found myself pursuing a doctorate degree in Public Administration at Virginia Tech through their graduate extension program. It was located at the Naval Surface Warfare Center in Dahlgren, Virginia, where I was still employed. I couldn't believe it, but there I was writing papers and studying for exams. I was the only person of color in class, most times the only woman, and not to mention I had a few years on most of my classmates as well. There were lots of men, highly educated white men who I figured would be smarter than me. After all, they went to better elementary and secondary schools, with better facilities and nice new books. And of course, they attended large, predominantly white institutions (PWIs) that I could only dream of attending when I applied to college at the undergraduate level.

I found out I was pretty smart, especially compared to some of my classmates who didn't know as much as I did. Some of them failed tests and were given the exams over so they could stay in the Ph.D. program. It was hard to believe that some had received degrees from prestigious white-only universities in the South, or PWIs in the north, and here they were being given second chances. I thought to myself that would never happen at dear ole Virginia State.

That's the thing about Historically Black Colleges and Universities (HBCUs) back in the day. They did not make it easy for us because part of their mission was to teach us more than just book knowledge. We were taught that we had to work twice as hard and learn more than our white counterparts to be competitive in the white-collar workforce. That went for blue-collar as well. Accordingly, they let us know when we set foot on campus that we were there to learn our classwork and learn how to compete. Those who did not get their work done because of a lack of effort were sent home. No makeup tests, no breaks, no ifs, ands or buts because they were preparing us for the harsh world of discrimination and prejudice that lie ahead of us. We were coming from HBCUs, trying to prove that we were as strong, bright, and prepared as the white students graduating from the very schools that ironically did not accept us because of our "colored" skin. Schools with those fancy initials like UVA, VCU, and oh, by the way, VPI, otherwise known as Virginia Tech.

The day my professor called me and said I had passed all my Ph.D. competencies with flying colors was memorable beyond words. I was so excited. I was working in my office at the end of a typically busy day, and when I received the good news, I was overcome with emotion. I wondered if I could even drive home safely because I was so excited. My husband Ira was retired and at home that afternoon. I just couldn't wait to tell him the good news in person, so I took a few deep breaths to calm myself down, and then in typical Gladys West fashion, I was on my way home, quick and in a hurry. It was probably the fastest that I've ever driven. Thank God I made it home safely, still on cloud nine, and in disbelief.

Ira must have thought something was wrong as I hurried to enter the house, nervously closing the door behind me. I was breathing hard and struggled to get the words out. Then I hear "What's wrong Gladys" from Ira more than once, and finally, I got the words out in between breaths "I did it, Ira, I did it." Then taking a deep breath before continuing, I explained, "My professor called and said I passed my competencies, and I'm going to be Doctor Gladys West!"

I had dreamed of this moment for an eternity, it seemed, and finally, it was no longer a dream; it was real. Ira smiled and calmed me down while gently hugging me against his chest. He was excited too, and probably relieved that I was gradually catching my breath and starting to breathe normally again. Ira knew I had accomplished not only a professional goal but something very personal that I had dreamed about almost all my life. Despite so many setbacks and challenges along the way, including a stroke in 1998 that could have left me unable to continue this doctoral pursuit, I had achieved my most important goal. Now, it was all over except for writing my dissertation, which I knew would be challenging as well, but not as difficult as passing those competencies. I felt so proud of this remarkable accomplishment not only for me but for all my family who had come before me. I would be the first to earn the Ph.D.

We celebrated quietly that night, Ira, and I, thanking God for this wonderful blessing, making phone calls to immediate family, reflecting on all that I had overcome, and pondering what it would feel like once I completed my dissertation. It was apparent that Ira was just as happy as I was, as he always is whenever I achieve something of significance. He has been the most supportive husband a woman could ask for. Yet, in his own protective way, he was probably praying that this would be the last time his wonderful wife would want to walk across a graduation stage. After all, I had earned a B.S., M.S., M.A., and now a Ph.D. was just a writing requirement away.

Earning that doctorate degree was my greatest academic or professional achievement, but it is the unlikely road I chose and path I traveled on this incredible journey that is the story I want to share with each of you, no matter your race, color, gender, age or walk of life. The adventure starts in a little town in rural Virginia, without a map, plan, or direction finder, at least not in the beginning anyway. This little girl who grew up poor, during the great depression, and in separate and "unequal" conditions proved again and again that success begins with a dream and a vision of what you want to accomplish in this amazing life, and that dream can only become a reality through faith, persistent work ethic, and a personal commitment to always be your best.

CHAPTER ONE: BUTTERWOOD

Most people say I have had a remarkably successful life, especially considering my educational achievements and long professional career as a mathematician, but clearly, it has been challenging to say the least, as I come from humble beginnings. On October 27, 1930, I was the second child that my parents, Nolan Brown, Sr., and Macy Pearl Brown brought into this world. It was a time of deprivation in rural, segregated Sutherland, Virginia at the beginning of The Great Depression. Life was no picnic for any of us, white or "colored", as they referred to us at that time. They named me Gladys Mae, and my brother who was about two and a half years older was named Joseph. My sister Annie and my younger brother Nolan, Jr. also came along about two years apart after us. Mama and Daddy did their best to provide for us the only way they knew how, with strong values, prayer, and an enduring work ethic.

My father was a farmer, working a small piece of land in a mostly poor community in Sutherland, Virginia, located in Dinwiddie County. It is a county known for its agricultural contributions, but most recognized as the home of the most battles during the American Civil War. The house I was raised in was not much to look at but was very typical for that time. It was a one-story Cape Cod looking frame structure with

7

an unfinished attic, no porch, and three or four wooden steps leading to the front door. In the front yard there was a towering, majestic oak tree that I adored; you know, the kind that provides lots of shade when you need some cooling off. We did not have air conditioning in those days, so it was nice and cool underneath that old tree in the summertime, especially after working in those hot steamy fields from sunup to sundown.

Nolan Brown, Sr., my daddy.

My mama, Macy Pearl Brown at a young age.

We had lots of chores every day on that farm and we were serious about our work especially since the family got paid for what was produced on the farm; there was no time for foolishness. We were a team, and everybody had to do their part, especially when my parents were busy doing other work outside of the farm. Our parents worked all the time, so quite often we had to take care of ourselves. As soon as I got old enough, maybe 10 or 11 years old, I would plant flowers near that big old oak after I finished my work, just to make things look nice and pretty. The blossoms were bright yellow with not much fragrance, so I think they may have been marigolds. The name of the flower did not matter though, I just had to do something to brighten things up because I am sure I got tired of looking at all those dirty and sometimes muddy fields that literally surrounded us and our home.

We lived in a densely wooded farming community just north of Highway 460, which ran mostly parallel to the railroad tracks, from east to west directly through Sutherland. Cox Road was close by on the east side of 460, not too far from what is now Interstate 85. Butterwood Road curled around from the south to connect with 460. There were fields, and trees as far as I could see. All the other houses around us were also on little pieces of farmland like ours. It was mostly flat land that had been cleared out by the men who headed their households and in some cases by the big tobacco men who owned most of the properties. The houses were very plain in style, similar to many of the small farmhouses that were prevalent in the Southern United States from the late 1800s through the 1930s. We were all fortunate though to have a roof over our heads, and that was something worth being thankful for, as our parents often reminded us.

My mother would often remind us that there were many people who did not have homes nor food to eat. She said we were blessed to have food every day and a nice dry place to sleep at night. Well it was dry most nights, but Mama meant well. She had a way of making you feel guilty when you started to complain about things. I still felt that we deserved better, like the people who lived in the so-called big cities, with paved streets, bright lights, and fancy shoes on their feet. I never did know or even meet people like that back then though. One or two of our neighbors had extended family members who visited from time to time, but they looked and sounded just as countrified as us, so I didn't pay them any mind.

I had heard about Richmond, our State Capital, but had never been there. A few times I overheard some people outside Olgers Store on Highway 460 talking about cities like Washington, DC, and New York, but I had no idea where they were located. It just seemed like they were millions of miles away. I figured they must be the places I was always dreaming about, where there would be no working in the fields, no wood chopping, and no tobacco harvesting, which was all we knew in our neck of the woods. I never met anybody from those important sounding places and had no clue what type of work they did, but I just imagined that they probably never got blisters on their hands or mud between their toes like me. I'm not sure what my sister and brothers were thinking, but in my mind, cities with names like that just sounded like places I wanted to be. All I knew was I wanted to find a way to get to one of those places someday, even if it took a month of Sundays to get there.

The first floor of our house consisted of a couple of rooms, one of which was a large room at the front of the house that doubled as a living room and our parents' bedroom. Behind it was another multi-purpose room, as your realtor may so eloquently refer to it today. It was complete with an annexed section that was a dining/kitchen area off to the side. A couple of roll-up beds for me and my siblings to share were also in that room. There was an upstairs to the house that was basically an attic, and there was a rickety old bed up there as well. My siblings and I would gather around the steps that led to the attic and play games sometimes, but it was very raw, hot, and stuffy up in that unfinished room, so it was not the most desirable place to hang out. No one wanted to be in that attic, especially on hot summer days when it felt like a sauna up there.

I remember on dreadfully hot days I would lay on the hardwood floors of the house because those floors always seemed to stay cool, compared to the air temperature inside the house. Once my siblings realized what I was doing, they started lying on the floor also, but they did not do it as much as I did. I always seemed a little different in that way. In the summer, the heat outside was suffocating at times, so we kept the windows to the house open, and every now and then you could feel a breeze at night. Those breezes were much more regular in the Spring and Fall, and it was wonderful to see those sheer curtains at our windows blowing freely as the breeze from outdoors gently cooled and refreshed the house. The cool fresh air coming through the windows was one of the benefits of living in rural, country places like Sutherland.

Conversely, the Winter seasons were harsh because though our weather was mild compared to some places north of us, it was difficult to stay warm in those old frame houses with no insulation and thin windowpanes. You can imagine just how much we depended on that overworked, but much appreciated wood stove. We always had to keep fire wood cut and stacked in the woodshed, because the wood stove was used to provide heat most of the year including to heat the straightening comb that my mama used to press/straighten me and my sister's hair; and heat our water. There was a large tin tub for taking baths. Yes, just one tub that sat at the rear of the house, near the roll-up beds. Bathing time was usually one day a week, and that day was Saturday in most households in the community. We would heat the water, fill the tub, and take our turn. Those Saturday baths were a luxury back then, considering most days we just rinsed off, you know, the bird bath way.

Mama cleaned clothes the old fashion way of course, which was an arduous and seemingly endless task back then. It was even more difficult on a farm because with all the physical labor required, we got dirty every day. We also had fewer clothes in our wardrobe making it necessary to wash clothes often. Modern detergents were not available until about the 1940s, so clothes were sorted out, and extra dirty items were left in galvanized dolly tubs overnight with some soap flakes added that we would purchase from the general store. White clothes would stand overnight in cold water that contained a bluish colored whitening agent, but we rarely had white clothes other than my dad's church shirts, so she did not have to bother with that process often.

She used washboards for scrubbing, and later a clothes mangle, hand operated machine consisting of two rollers to squeeze out excess water. Then we had to hang the clothes out on a clothesline to dry or lay them over a rack inside the house. I absolutely loved the fresh smell of my dresses after being out on that line to dry. Ironing was a laborious process as well, as irons were made of cast iron with a flat base and a handle. The iron would have to be heated over fire, thus another need for firewood. We had a couple of irons so she could have one iron heating while she was using the other. All this work never seemed to faze her though, and she continually worked hard to keep our clothes as clean as possible. I pitched in whenever I could to help Mama, especially with sorting the clothes and preparing them before washing and hanging the clothes to dry, but she was the real pro, no question about it. She handled the difficult tasks, which, as I remember, was an amazing sight to see.

I wore dresses every day because that's what girls did. Women and girls wouldn't dare wear pants even while working at home or in the fields. My shoes were very much basic and were made to withstand the wear from the very physical farming work. I had this one pair of brown oxford shoes that my mother had bought from the store without me being there, so those shoes were too short and hurt my feet. I begged to keep them because I thought they were so nice. She let me keep them but whenever I wore them, I'm sure I had the look of pain on my face. I was happy though and just forced out a few smiles somehow. I also had one pair of fancy patent leather shoes, but they were for church only. I re-member there was this blue dress that I liked most, and of course I did not wear it when I was cutting or stacking wood and working in the field. That dress was for school and church only, so it never got too dirty. Luckily, we only went to church once a month though because the Church that we attended had to share the preacher with several other churches in the county. Therefore, those shoes and that pretty little dress lasted longer since I did not wear them every week.

My favorite thing was to take my good clothes off after school and change into my older clothes that were near worn out and were not thought of as "away from home" clothes. We had an aunt who would periodically send us a box of old clothes that we only wore at home and in the fields. Even when I wore those old worn out dresses I just fit in with the other kids, because it was just the way it was for poor folks who lived in rural areas at that time and you just accepted it. It was a different world back in those days.

One of my special memories of the old house is that it had a tin roof and sometimes during periods of rain, I would lay there on the floor and listen to the rhythmic, melodic sounds of the raindrops continuously falling on that old roof. In my mind, it sounded like a song or a jazz composition or something. It was sort of magical and always one of my favorite things to do during a rainstorm. I had to find things like that to help me get through the days of feeling bad about my day to day life on that farm. It helped to have that kind of imagination, and of course, thank goodness for that old tin roof with its magical songs that I still remember on quiet rainy days today.

There were three sheds on our property. One for stacking wood, another for storing Mama's canned and preserved foods, and yes you guessed it, the third shed was the outhouse. Just in case you don't know, that's where you had to go to do your business. We tried to keep it as clean as possible, though there wasn't much you could do with an old wooden outhouse. We had these big ceramic pots that we kept cleaned out and stored in the house during the day, and for night-time situations that often arose if you had to relieve yourself in the middle of the night. Going outside to that shed in the pitch-black darkness under those country skies was something I tried to avoid. They say "black holes" are true to their name, and are the darkest things in the universe, but those experts never visited my ole neighborhood at midnight in mid to late December. Comparing it to the vast reaches of the universe might be stretching it a bit, but in my mind the darkest skies on earth were right there in little Dinwiddie County.

Every family had a couple of those chamber pots, otherwise known in the country as "pee pots" that they kept in the house. Our jars were a pretty chocolate brown color, which from my recollection was the most popular color in the neighborhood. Yes, having no indoor plumbing was a very humbling experience, but again, we didn't know anything different. I sometimes wonder how we were able to make it in that little house. I dreamed of one day living somewhere bigger, prettier, and different, but the dreams were vague because I had not been anywhere outside of Sutherland, and only a few times to Petersburg with my Daddy when he delivered the tobacco we had harvested. I had nothing to reference to give me realistic ideas and visions of what it would be like somewhere else. I kept dreaming though and using my wonderful imagination.

Most of the neighbors in the area had large families. All similarly situated, hard-working people, mostly farmers and some did unskilled work at the tobacco plant over in Petersburg. There was only one black man who worked fulltime for the railroad, keeping the tracks maintained and so forth, so his family had just a little bit more than everyone else. The stores and businesses were all mostly located along Highway 460 or Cox Road. They were owned by white families, and although we did not go to schools with their children, we knew them rather well because our parents patronized their stores, shops, and gasoline stations.

There was one store that my father would purchase most of the things that we needed, so he became good friends with the owner, Mr. Olgers. Daddy was a relatively small, thin man, always clean cut, with no mustache or beard, so I guess he never looked intimidating to the white men. They always seemed to enjoy his company up at the store, as far as I could tell from the outside. You see I always had to stay in the car with my mother and my sister while my father and my brothers went inside the store to pick up the things we needed to purchase. I assume Daddy thought that it was not the proper place for a female at that time in our country, especially in Dinwiddie County, Virginia. I do remember the owner's children playing outside the store and coming over to the car and speaking to me and my sister. They were a little younger than me, but I always enjoyed talking to them and watching them play while waiting for Daddy and my brothers. I still know one of the owner's sons to this day, as he's still there in Sutherland running that store, which is now filled with antiques.

The normal day for me and my siblings consisted of getting up in the morning and doing whatever work had to be done around the house and the yard. It seems that chopping wood was the most needed chore, and the most hated by me. We had to go into the woods, down below the back of the house, just before you get to a small ravine. We would then pick out an old or dead tree that daddy had cut down and saw it with one of those two handled crosscut saws (handle on both ends). This was the kind of saw used for cutting large logs back in the day, but it has been replaced mostly by power chain saws today. Here I was, this little girl doing what needed to be done. I took the lead often because my brother, who was very playful, would try to get away from working hard, so I would get one end of that saw and tell him to grab the other end. Together we would start sawing away, back and forth with push/pull strokes in each direction until we cut the logs down to size and into firewood. Then we had to bring it to the woodshed and stack it for use in the wood stove and for other purposes that required split wood.

We also raised a few chickens, cows, and hogs, so we fed them each day too. Daddy wanted Joseph and Nolan, Jr. to slop the hogs and to help him with the old farm horses, teaching them how to be men and all. Nolan, Jr. was the younger of the two, so he didn't expect much from him, but Joseph always seemed to mess up something especially when trying to manage those horses. He would be chasing one of the horses, and slipping and falling in the mud, and my sister and I just couldn't stop laughing; it was often our weekly entertainment. Poor Daddy would shout, "Boy, what are you doing with my horse" and just shake his head, both in disbelief and disappointment, but every now and then he would see Joseph lying on the ground covered in mud and he just couldn't help but laugh along with us. Yes indeed, that Joseph was something else.

On school days, my brothers, my sister, and I would routinely meet up with some of the other kids as we made our way to school. Some of them were our cousins the Jeffersons who lived across the road. Morris Jefferson was my favorite cousin because he was big and strong and would protect us from some of the bad kids that liked to start fights. Freddie was the same age as my older brother and Arlene was my age. Then there were James and Harold, our other cousins, who were our walking partners as well. Their house was directly across the road, and we picked up Charlie Brown, George Thomas, and a few other cousins along the way, but I cannot remember all the other names, except

17

Dorothy Mae, whose daughter still attends Rocky Branch Baptist Church in Sutherland today.

We walked, skipped, and laughed those three miles each way to and from school every day. It seems none of us were ever sick, and if we were, we went to school anyway. Along the way, we quickly encountered the railroad train tracks that ran parallel to the main highway in Sutherland. We crossed them easily, with some of the boys showing off by leaping across as if broad jumping. I was rather prissy, especially in my "away from home" clothes, so I stepped across those big old tracks as graceful as a princess. Arlene and my sister Annie would follow me in the same fashion. Our next adventure was to cross Highway 460, so we had to be mindful of cars traveling on this two-lane main road through town. The good thing is that cars were not too fast in the 1930s and 40s, so we could handle getting to the other side with no problem. Then we would follow this little dirt road, that no longer exists, until we reached Butterwood Road. Along the way, there was nothing but woods and farmland, and some big farms too, with horses, cows, and corn as high as we were tall.

Before long we would arrive at Butterwood Road School. It was the school for "colored" in our parts that housed children from first grade through seventh grade. A one-room, off-white colored building, close to the road, that probably was white initially, but was perhaps in need of a fresh paint job. There were lots of tall pines all around and a couple of big oaks, as grand as the one at my house. Inside there were tables spread across the creaky, wooden floors, with old benches that we sat on, two to three of us to a bench. Our teacher was Mrs. Ledbetter, and she was tasked with teaching all the grades and dealing with kids of varying ages.

I still don't know how she did it, but I do remember that she did seem to sit the younger kids closer to her, and the older ones on the other side of the room. I'm sure that Normal School that she attended prepared her well because we all seemed to do well in life despite what we had to go through to get an education. The books were second hand, worn and sometimes missing pages. The furniture was old; and some looked to be falling apart. There was a large wood stove inside though, which kept us warm throughout the winter. The bigger boys would take turns toting the firewood inside as needed.

During the school day, we had to ask the teacher to go to the bathroom, which was an outhouse, in the woods and quite a distance from the school, maybe 100 feet away. It had two holes, a two-seater, and on some hot days when the schoolhouse was downwind, it was probably a good thing that old outhouse was tucked away so far from us. We had a recess break each day and we played ball a little bit. Hopscotch and marbles were our other favorites. No lunch was provided at the school, so Mama always packed lunches for us. I can't remember for sure, but I think it was mostly cheese and cold cuts, because we didn't know anything about peanut butter and jelly back then.

Mrs. Ledbetter, a tall, big woman, reminded me somewhat of George Washington because of her hairstyle and I always joked about it with my friends. She appeared to be in her late thirties to early forties when I was at Butterwood. She was really good with home economics and took a lot of time teaching me and some of the other girls about cooking and sewing and things like that. One thing she couldn't do well was sing, so she never taught us much about music, so that's one reason I believe I can't sing today. She was always fond of me though because

I was attentive, always did my work, and was one of the better-behaved children at Butterwood. I never wanted to disappoint my parents, so I was always a good student and as a result, always stood out.

One year a family with several school-age children moved in next to our farm; and their children would walk to school with us. Tobacco was king at that time in Dinwiddie County, so this family had moved to Sutherland from North Carolina to be hired hands for the enormous tobacco farming companies in the area. The big, white-owned farming businesses brought people up from South Carolina and North Carolina to take care of their crops and harvest the tobacco. They were basically sharecroppers, who were provided a roof over their heads, and some land to farm the tobacco crop and to raise food for their families.

Some of these businessmen had several families doing the farming for them, and the tobacco they harvested was the property of these large farming businesses that were providing the bulk of the tobacco to the tobacco and cigarette companies in Petersburg and Richmond. It was late and post-depression, but the cigarette industry was still fairly productive. Those Carolina kids turned out to be some of the bad kids in the neighborhood and at school. I often wondered why they didn't take too kindly to us, especially since we were all people of color, and all in this thing together. I guess they were feeling the pain of the way they had been treated all their lives by white folks, and maybe even night riders as they called them. They could have been just taking out their frustrations on any and everybody because of some unthinkable things they had witnessed being born black in the South. They were always trying to pick a fight about something, but it was nothing my big cousin Morris couldn't handle, so I always felt safe and secure playing in the neighbor-hood and walking to and from Butterwood School.

That's the road I walked most days. It was comfortable, familiar and I could navigate its twists, turns, bumps, and oh yes, those railroad train tracks with my eyes closed. The sweet fragrance of the honey-suckle, and the fresh, distinctive smell of the tall pines I knew so well. I even knew the bugs, the birds, and the bees that I greeted daily. I'd say, "Good morning Mr. Bumble Bee. You're mighty busy I see, and morn-ing Miss Butterfly, now don't you fly away without me." Sometimes I think they understood what I was saying too, but those bugs and bees were content with being in the country. It was perfect for them, plenty of grass, trees, flowers, open space, and fresh air, but if they had to work on that farm like me, they would not be so happy. They would want to fly away to the city just like me. I also counted fenceposts along the road and across the fields as we walked to school, just to have something dif-ferent to do. I became good at it, never realizing that I was sharpening some skills and abilities that I would one day utilize to help calculate the hypothetical shape of the earth. Who would have thought it as that road with no way out just seemed like the path that was set out for me and my folks from the beginning of time. It was the only way of life around there. Farming, harvesting, working for white folks, and struggling to make ends meet, day after endless day without ever catching up. If you were "colored" the only exceptions to that reality were the teacher and the preacher.

Before I reached adolescence, I had already realized that my thoughts were different from many of the other children. I absolutely knew I had to get away from that farm. I also realized I could not do domestic work, nor toil in that smelly, disgusting tobacco plant as my mother and the other women of color in our community had endured their entire lives. Interestingly enough, I learned a lot from the older ladies I watched every day when I was growing up. They were not very educated and did not hold any titles, other than wife, mother, and grandmother. Still, just by watching them, I learned a lot about organization and planning and taking care of the things that needed to be done to keep their families together in hard times. It was a characteristic I saw in many of those women. They were strong, stern, concerned women who took care of their families. I could tell many of them were the leaders of their households, and despite having limited resources and finances, these ladies were masters of keeping things afloat.

I especially admired my Mama for the way she went about her daily grind. She was a role model for me in the sense that she was profoundly serious about everything she did. There were those times when mama and daddy would be giggling together and showing affection, which made me smile, but she was generally extremely focused, and always prepared for the future. She made sure we canned and preserved, dried, and salted down, and did everything that had to be done so that we had food throughout the year and especially during the winter months. The way she kept our clothes clean and the house tidy was remarkable, and not to mention keeping me and my sister's hair done every day when we were young, which was not an easy feat. You see, our hair was not as easy to comb through as hers. We took hair after my daddy's side. It was thicker and coarser than mama's hair, but she did it with a smile and never complained, and she told us how pretty we looked after she finished. She always made us feel so beautiful. Even when we were doing our chores, she called us her little princesses, and that meant a lot to us. Her organizational and planning skills were impeccable, but more importantly, she was a warm and giving woman, and concerned about her family, and seemingly anyone else she was in contact with regularly.

I spent a lot of time with her and remember how she was always reaching out to her siblings whenever they were in trouble or needed money, which, unfortunately, was quite often. She always helped them however she could, not as a favor but as if it were an obligation because they were her kinfolk. Sometimes she got paid back and sometimes she didn't, but I think she felt that it was the right thing to do and that was all that mattered. I also recall her taking care of a neighbor's little girl one day who had some really, thick, hard to manage hair. Mama painstakingly worked on that child's hair for hours until she got it exactly right. She made sure that little girl was pleased. That's the way she handled everything, always putting other people first, and never doing anything halfway. That little girl's mother brought her back to our house a few more times after seeing the care she got from Macy Brown, and frankly, I don't blame that child's mother at all.

Even now, I have a thing for organization and laying out plans, which is something that really helped me as a professional in math and science, and in leadership roles. Oddly enough, I learned it first from my mama and those older black ladies back in Sutherland, not from any textbook. I picked it up just watching and emulating the qualities and skills of those amazing women. Although I didn't want to do farm or domestic work, I wanted to be like them. I think mama could see that she was my idol. I believe she saw herself in me. It appeared she thought I could do no wrong. Yes sir, the sun rose and set with her Gladys Mae. I wasn't perfect, but in her eyes, I was the next best thing to sliced bread. She always made such a fuss over me when some of the other ladies were around. I always made good grades in school, never gave teachers any trouble in school, and Mama was so proud about that, but what she really liked was the way I helped her around the house and out in the field. I had learned how to be accountable at a very young age. "I can always count on Gladys Mae, she never gives me any trouble," she would say, and that was as important to her as anything in the world. I always thought the world of her too, and just as she could count on me, I could always count on her as well.

I had visions about other ways of making a living that stretched my boundless imagination. Where those dreams came from, I have no idea. It's not like I saw it on television. There was no television, and lord knows I didn't have any books with ideas like that lying around the house. Books were scarce. However, the thought of being on that farm, breaking my back, surrounded by tobacco fields the rest of my days on this earth was a frightening one. The older I became, the more I felt locked into the reality that I may never have an opportunity to experience a different way of life. I always made the best of my days, though, by continuing to dream and imagine that I would be doing some other kind of work when I grew up.

I didn't understand at that time in my life why people who looked like us worked so much harder than others, yet always stayed poor. It just didn't seem fair. Now don't get me wrong, I loved the peace and quiet, and the country living in my hometown. However, I knew if the opportunity presented itself for me to move on, I would not hesitate to widen my horizons, and I certainly wasn't going to worry about it.

Although that old country road I walked countless times was all I knew, there just had to be another road. A road with no end, one that would stir up my imagination, encourage me to dream often, and give me the strength to passionately chase those dreams. If there was such a road, I had to either find it or pave it myself.

Similar to the railroad tracks we crossed on the way to school.

My sister Annie on the left and me on the right.

My hard-working daddy.

From left to right, Nolan, Jr., Me, and Annie.

CHAPTER TWO: FINDING THE ROAD LESS TRAVELED

During my last years at the Butterwood School, our great American society, as we knew it, was being threatened. We were finally recovering from the long, harsh effects of the Great Depression when Nazi Germany's Adolph Hitler began his quest to build an empire by invading and defeating Poland. Then on December 7, 1941, Japan's surprise attack on Pearl Harbor forced President Franklin D. Roosevelt and Congress to declare war on Japan. Roosevelt famously called that attack a "day of infamy." Germany and Italy responded by declaring war on America, thus throwing us into a second World War. There was global fighting and destruction going on involving more than 30 countries. These were scary times for Americans. Whether you were white, colored, from the big urban areas, or rural folks like ourselves, the war tested the souls of our greatest generation, and even if only for a few years, we came together to defeat these nations that seemed so evil, which probably was the most epic challenge ever to America and to the world. The way Americans reacted to the 9/11 terrorist attack on the World Trade Center Buildings and the Pentagon reminded me of how shocking and devastating the Pearl Harbor attack was, and how it brought all the people together. That American pride kicked in it seemed, and no matter your color or ethnic background, there was only one team that mattered, and it was the Red, White, and Blue.

Uncle Sam was everybody's uncle now, and it was interesting to see "Colored" folks being so "patriotic," a word that would matter to me and remain solidly in my vocabulary for life. I was now about 11 years old and had never seen so many colored men and women so loyally defending the same America that had subjected them to discrimination, segregation, and Jim Crow laws all their lives. Many of our boys were signing up to fight, just like the white boys, despite the armed forces still being segregated as well. Can you imagine going off to war to fight for a country that wouldn't even let you fight alongside your white peers? Now that's patriotic.

Quite often, we would hear our parents and the other adults discussing the war and the economy, but when children were near, you could hear their voices soften so that we couldn't understand what they were talking about, almost as if they were saying bad words. Like the way adults spelled out words and whispered words that they did not think were appropriate for minors, or youngins as they use to say. Then they would change the subject and mention how nice the weather had been the last few days. Parents tended to be like that because they thought we might get stressed out, but we knew what was going on, especially with so many of our young men joining the military and not being around anymore. Our teacher, Mrs. Ledbetter also talked about it a few mornings after we did the pledge of allegiance, and you know she threw in a few "Lord's Prayers" as well. Some boys said we had to win like Joe Louis beat Smelling. Not to mention seeing those young soldiers, all uniformed up and high spirited that we passed by many times on our way to school.

I found out later that those soldiers were from Fort Lee, an Army base located in Petersburg, Virginia, not far from Sutherland. They would camp out on bivouac, an overnight military exercise where they would practice for situations that they may encounter in the war. At first, it was quite intimidating to see these dozens of soldiers camped out with all that equipment, right in our backyard almost. It was a frightening thing to see them that way, so in the beginning, we stayed away from them, and they just went about their work. We eventually waved to them sometimes, and they just threw their hands up instinctively, but with not much emotion. Those guys were on a mission, and they took it very seriously. My brother Joseph, the practical joker that he was, saluted the soldiers one morning for fun, and a couple of them surprisingly saluted back and said something like, "Come join us. We have a uniform for you." Well, they scared Joseph so bad it was the last time he bothered them or even looked their way. My brother knew he was no match for those guys. He could no more stand up to those guys than he could to daddy's old farm horses.

That war made us grow up fast. At age eleven, going on twelve, I could sense that it was a difficult time in America. However, our parents did not talk about it much. Fortunately, my father was a little too old and had four young children, so he never had to leave us and serve in that old war. I often wondered, however, what it must have felt like for those young soldiers camping out in the woods near Butterwood Road while waiting their turn to go and fight for our country. It appeared that some of them were not that much older than Morris or Joseph. I wonder if some of the troops that we saw and waved to as we made our way to school those days were sent into action; and how many of them never returned home. The war lasted until 1945, and I was in high school by then. Two atomic bombs had been dropped on Japan, the only use of nuclear weapons ever in war. As I went about my life in rural Virginia, the world was experiencing the deadliest conflict in human history. The war came, and to everyone's relief, it went, yet things still seemed the same in Sutherland. We lost a few of our young men who were casualties of the war, but there was nothing else different, especially for poor "colored" folks like us. Uncle Sam had defeated Nazi-Germany's Hitler and Japan's Hirohito, but allowed old Jim Crow to remain very much alive right here on our own home soil – So despite our uncompromising loyalty and patriotism to democracy and this country, life just continued onward for many of us, with no more hope and opportunities than before.

I was into my high school experience then and began to see more clearly that there was a life beyond the tobacco fields of Sutherland, Virginia. It opened my eyes to new ideas, new possibilities, and a new appreciation for my favorite subject, mathematics. I wasn't that crazy about algebra, and I did not fully master it, but geometry was something that just came naturally to me, with the help of one of the best teachers I ever knew. I was starting to realize early that this newly found love for geometry was something that could help me find that road I had dreamed about, the road that would take me far away from that farm. The road not often traveled by folks where I was from.

I had moved from the little one-room schoolhouse with one teacher for seven years to the Dinwiddie Training School for Colored, with different classrooms and several teachers for all the grade levels, so clearly, there was an adjustment period. We even had a librarian who helped us develop an appreciation for reading. There were also buses that carried us to the school about 17 miles from Sutherland. It was exciting to be in high school, although the name "training school" did not sound very academic, but that was the least to complain about back then.

This is where I met Mr. Lee, who taught geometry and was a very bright and scholarly man. Although he taught us to be very serious about our studies, he also had a way of making the lessons enjoyable. I became fascinated with geometry, particularly how he related it to everyday life. He even related it to farming, such as measuring the inclines of the land, and how the knowledge of angles and degrees could possibly make a farmer's job easier. I learned to have a better appreciation for the work we did on the farm from Mr. Lee, but don't get me wrong, he still never convinced me that a lifetime of those hot, sweaty days in the field was for me. It was nice to know that those farms and the people who worked them may be the backbone of America, but I figured there had to be other ways of being patriotic, and besides, I was convinced that wearing "away from home clothes" every day was definitely in my future.

I enjoyed my high school years and became more aware of my interest and aptitude in math and science, so between studying, cutting wood, feeding the chickens, and helping Mama with housework, I stayed busy. I probably should have relaxed or played around with the other kids, but it just always seemed like there was something to do around the house that I could do to help my parents, and that was always important to me. Playing and socializing with my friends and classmates was not a priority – Being the best student and best daughter was, so I did not so-cialize as much as I probably should have.

As I approached my last year at Dinwiddie Training School, I began to hear that I was college material from Mr. Lee and some of the other teachers. I apparently had some of the highest grades in my class, and it was time to think about how I was going to get into college. My teachers were recommending that I consider applying to the Norfolk campus of Virginia State College (now Norfolk State University), Virginia Union, and Virginia State College, all (HBCUs) in the State of Virginia, but I told them we didn't have any money for college. Nobody in my family had been to college, and I only knew of one other person in my community who had gone. Dorothy Bates was her name, and she was a couple years older than me. I did not know her very well until we became adults, but when I was in school, I admired her from a distance. She was a role model and did not realize it. I heard from a very wise man that unless you are invisible, you are a role model to someone. It could be in a negative or positive way, but if you can be seen or heard, you are a role model. That was never truer than it was with the way Dorothy had an influence on me. She was different from the other farm girls. I watched how she handled herself and how she was always serious about her schoolwork, and I wanted to be like her. I actually think she may have noticed me following in her path, and was challenging me, not verbally, but by her actions, "Come on, Gladys, you can do this too." Dorothy passed away the Summer of 2018, and I was there at her homegoing service to show my respects, and to thank her one more time for being one of my first role models. I was blessed to have someone who looked just like me that I could look up to, and pattern myself after.

I wanted to follow Dorothy so badly and go off to college myself. She was already at Virginia State in Petersburg, and I hoped that I could go there too, but where was I going to get the money? I worked extremely hard to do the best I could, hoping that I would be noticed by someone who could help me get into college. I studied hard and was so prepared for tests that I would finish them sometimes in one third the time of the other students. I kept pushing myself, day by day, month by month, then one day, a counselor at school told me that if I could finish first or second in my class that I could earn a scholarship to college in the State of Virginia. I was elated to hear that, and now I had to figure out who my competition was and work harder than that person.

It turned out that there was only one other person that I would have to compete with, and I became friends with her. She and I worked together and pushed each other for the rest of our senior year, and even though I only had to finish second in the class, in my heart, I wanted to finish first, always wanting to be the best. I remember when the principal told me I had finished first in the class. I was so happy, and now my dream of going to college was closer to coming true. There was still one thing to figure out though. As things go, the scholarship was for tuition only and did not include room and board. Virginia State was the closest college to us, but I would still have to stay on campus. My parents could not really afford it, but Mama said she did not want me to work the first year so I could concentrate on my schoolwork. She and Daddy agreed to somehow pay for me to stay on campus that first year. So I was going to college, and nothing could stop me now.

Before long, I was feeling all grown up and leaving for Virginia State College. It was exciting but nerve-racking as well. I would have to meet new friends and become accustomed to being away from home also. I wasn't going to miss all that farm work, but I would miss my parents and my sister and brothers, my cousins, and even those bad kids from North Carolina who had moved down the road, especially since they had calmed down somewhat by now, thanks to my big cousin

Morris. I was thinking how much I would miss keeping cool under that big oak tree in the front yard, and the musical sounds of the raindrops falling on our tin roof, and those cool breezes blowing through the front windows in the Fall. Chopping wood, harvesting tobacco, and feeding the chickens, well, that wasn't going to be missed at all, and I wasn't going to give it a second thought either because now I was a college girl, a Virginia State Trojan, moving into Byrd Hall.

When my parents carried me over to the campus and left me there for the first time, it was extremely difficult for us all. It seemed there were teardrops on our living room floor as big as those raindrops that would leak through that old tin roof during a big rainstorm. It was bad enough for me in my heart to leave home, but Mama was worse off than I was. We were very close, and it was the first time that we were going to be apart. Remember, I was also the first in my family to attend college. She cried and cried after she got me all squared away in my dorm room before returning home to Sutherland. The campus was less than ten miles from Sutherland, but on that day, as she left me standing alone on the Byrd Hall steps, reluctantly preparing to drive home without me, it probably felt like she would be a thousand miles away. Daddy hugged me and then comforted Mama as he helped her into the truck. At that moment, I knew I would be seeing her often, and sure enough, most Saturdays I would get a visit and a "care package" from Mama and Daddy. Her excuse was she wanted to make sure I was getting enough to eat. As I said before, we had a big vegetable garden, and lots of chickens, so the Browns always ate good.

Freshman year was one of big transition, and particularly challenging, but I was determined to show that I belonged there. There was one thing I knew, and it was that I had to do it all by myself, without my parents and without Mrs. Ledbetter or Mr. Lee. One thing you learn fast in college is that the professors are not going to hold your hand, and you have to grow up fast. I had two roommates, Winifred, and Florence, but to my amazement, I had my own bed for the first time in my young life. I felt blessed, but when I thought about it, my younger sister Annie who I shared that roll out bed with, now had her own bed as well, so I am sure she enjoyed that too.

I was majoring in mathematics, one of the most difficult majors on campus, and the classes were hard, so I had to be more conscientious about my studies to maintain the mandatory grade point average that was necessary to keep the scholarship. Without the scholarship, I would be back in Sutherland working on that farm, and I prayed every night that I would never have to do that again. As the semester went by, there was an occasional athletic event that was mandatory for freshmen to attend, and that was quite different for me because we didn't have any sports teams or bands at my high school. Virginia State had all the sports and a very good band, but football was the most popular because that's when we had homecoming. I knew nothing about football, so there I was watching the games with my roommates, not having any idea what was going on. I just watched those big boys push, pull, and throw each other to the ground. When our fans would stand up, I stood up, and when they cheered, I cheered, but I had no idea why. I think we had a pretty good team, though, because we were standing up and cheering a lot. I enjoyed watching the band the most, just watching them majestically high step into Rogers Stadium drew more cheers than the game itself and left us with cherished memories.

I didn't do a lot of partying and socializing like some of the other students that I knew. I wasn't sure if I could do that and still get good grades. Some of the students on campus were from large urban areas, like Richmond and Norfolk, and they were better prepared for college. I, on the other hand, was a little behind them because I had not been exposed to much at all other than farm animals and tobacco fields, but I wasn't going to complain. I just had to focus on my goals and put in the work. There were some students who were followers and tried to socialize with the big city students who were having fun, but they were not from strong educational backgrounds, so they failed.

Thank goodness I wasn't the partying type, so it did not bother me so much not to hang out, but I sometimes wonder if I missed out by not having much of a social life back then. I went to class and studied, and then studied some more. My grades were okay, not straight A's like I was accustomed to in high school, but I grew a lot that year as a student. I also grew in inches around the waist, too, between not missing any meals each day at the campus dining hall; and those Ma Macy care packages two or three times a month. My roommates and I were enjoying the fried chicken, collard greens, and sweet potato pies that filled those packages, and by second semester we were becoming quite pleasingly plump might I say, but it didn't bother us so much since we entered college a little on the thin side. We maintained our figures, though, by quickly adjusting to the new life, and thank goodness we did not receive those Ma Macy care packages all four years.

Freshman year and throughout my time at Virginia State, I learned a lot about life, the world, and about the history and culture of our people. I was introduced to the great work and contributions of leaders such as, DuBois, Douglas, Tubman, Booker T. Washington, Mary McLeod Bethune, and some of the contemporary intellectuals at that time like Howard University President, Mordecai Johnson, and Lincoln University alumnus, Langston Hughes. It was fascinating, and I was blessed to be taught by some of the brightest minds in mathematics and the sciences, who were right there at Virginia State. These prominent educators inspired and encouraged us to learn and be the best we could be. As was generally the case at HBCUs, they cared for us like we were family, and they gave us opportunities to develop our leadership skills and abilities while encouraging us to be advocates for justice. There was a commitment to our communities and to underserved populations that was so prevalent on these campuses back in the day. We developed not only academically but personally and socially. It was an experience we all benefited from, and I only regret that I did not get involved more with some of the student-led organizations on campus.

During my second year at Virginia State, I began working for Drs. John and E. Louise Hunter. A married couple extraordinaire, they were both educators and highly intellectual, or what my Ma Macy called "book smart." I had an opportunity to move out of the dorm and live with the Hunters as well. They had a home on campus as did a few other tenured professors, which was common, especially at historically black colleges at that time. My job was to help them keep the house tidy and be a sitter for their young daughter, Jean. I had free room and board, and for the first time in my young life, I had my own bedroom. I also had two built-in role models of the highest distinction. As it happens, the usual college dorm life for the remainder of my undergraduate years was over, but that wasn't my style anyway. Sometimes I reflect on those days and wish I had more fun hanging out with my classmates, but I was not a real social person and not much of a party girl. The peace and quiet of the Hunter home where I could focus more on my studies was perfect for me, and besides, they had much better food in the fridge than what was available at the campus dining hall. Thus, Ma Macy's care packages, especially the eatable variety, came much less frequently.

It has become more apparent to me recently that being around this "power couple" was a blessing, although I did not realize it at the time. John Hunter was a physicist, chemist, educator, and administrator. Born in Woodville, Texas, he did as much as any single individual in this country to increase the amount of African American students to the professional rosters of physicists. He had received a B.S. in Electrical Engineering from Massachusetts Institute of Technology (MIT), and an M.S. in Physics from Cornell University and conducted research in the area of thermionics (relating to the emission of electrons by an incandescent material). He started the Physics Department at Virginia State, served as a Professor, and was the first Chairperson of the newly created department. While at Cornell University in 1937, he became the third African American in the U.S. to earn a Ph.D. in Physics. Dr. Hunter was highly respected at Virginia State, joining Dr. T. Nelson Baker, Jr. (Chemistry) and Dr. Rueben R. McDaniel (Mathematics), and other professors to build programs in Science, Technology, Engineering, and Math, now called STEM, on our campus. He was not the first college educated person in his family, as his mother was an educator - a home economics professor at Virginia State.

His wife, Dr. E. Louise Stokes Hunter, was a wonderful woman and taught mathematics at State. She had B.S. and M.S. degrees in

Mathematics, both from Howard University. I was in her math class the second semester of my freshman year and told her I would be looking for a job on campus when I came back in the Fall of my sophomore year. She said that she may need someone and would consider me for the job. Then she came out to the house to meet my parents and tell them she was thinking about hiring me. We never had a visitor at the house that looked like her before, in that pretty dress, and shiny car. My daddy had even taken off his dirty overalls and freshened up when he found out she was visiting. She explained that I would be working and living at her home on campus. Ma Macy thought it was a great idea and told her everything. She said, "one thing about Gladys, she doesn't have a lazy bone in her body." I thought to myself, "Why is Mama telling her everything about me," but I also thought, "I know I have the job now" because Mama made it seem like I could walk on water. The Hunters offered me the job that next day. Mrs. Hunter also had one of the boys on campus wash her car the next day, too, after all that dirt and dust it had accumulated at our little place in the country. I made a mental note - *Take Ma Macy on future job interviews.*

I began my sophomore year working for the Hunters, and while I was living with them, Louise Hunter began working on her doctorate degree. She and fellow Virginia State faculty member Walter Ridley entered the University of Virginia (UVA) at about the same time seeking to make history. She took me with her to Charlottesville a few times to look after Jean, while she attended class and visited the library on the UVA campus. I did not realize history was being made, but I was there with her almost the entire time she was working on that degree. In August 1953, she became the first African American woman and second

African American period to graduate with a degree from UVA. Ridley graduated a few months before her, becoming the first African American to graduate from UVA. By that time, I had graduated from Virginia State and had a teaching job. I remember it all too well, and I'm sure living amongst such scholars, who were doing historical things, had an immense impact on me at that very significant time in my life.

Since I worked and lived with the Hunters, I had no bills to pay for school my last three years. My tuition was covered by my four-year scholarship, and now I did not have to pay room and board. *Hallelujah*, I thought to myself, *God was looking out for me*. I felt extremely blessed, and I was so grateful that they hired me because my parents did not have any more money for me. I did not have to look for a part-time job somewhere like most of the other students. All I had to do was stay in good standing academically to keep the tuition scholarship, do my work at the Hunter home, and I would graduate in four years with no money owed to Virginia State.

This would prove to be another blessing and life-changing experience for me because I was able to concentrate more on my studies, and I was able to observe these two amazing individuals. I had never known black folks who were so accomplished, intelligent, and so fancy. They didn't even have overalls or any kind of clothes you could wear in the field, and even their fingernails were always clean. It seemed like they had never lived in the conditions I had come from, although they obviously had.

I'm not sure where Louise Hunter was born, but John Hunter was born in Woodville, Texas, a small town known only for its annual Dogwood Festival, and for being the hometown of Zelmo Beaty, a basketball star at historically black Prairie View A & M, an NBA center with the old St. Louis Hawks, and a member of the 1971 American Basketball Association (ABA) champion Utah Stars. At 6'11", Beaty may have been the largest man in stature from Woodville, but Dr. Hunter, large in stature himself, is arguably the most accomplished person from that town, although he is not recognized as such. Hunter was achieving things at a time in history that very few people, black or white, had even thought about. This from a black man born in 1901, in a segregated, "one-horse" town with a population of roughly 600, in East Texas that was as small and country as Sutherland.

It was hard to imagine, but it helped me to realize that I should continue to dream and aspire to be great like them. If the Hunters could do it, so could I, if I wanted it bad enough. When I first met them, I often wondered where they were from and thought, surely not from Dinwiddie County. They must have been from that place I always dreamed about. However, they were just regular black folks from similar roots who came into my life, and if I paid attention, maybe now, they could show me how to find the road I was searching for if I weren't already on that road.

They didn't ask much from me, but I always wondered, when would I be asked to go out and chop some wood or pull weeds from the garden. Thankfully, that day never came because I had left all my farm clothes at home in Sutherland, praying I would never have use for them anymore. I assisted them with household duties, such as tidying the living room, dining area, and kitchen, and washing dishes. I also helped keep the floors swept, furniture dusted, and the windows clean. I cooked for them as well, and at first, I was afraid that I could not cook the kind of meals that they would want since I only knew how to cook the way we cooked in the country.

They were sophisticated folks, so I asked Mrs. Hunter to teach me how to cook some things that she and Dr. Hunter liked. That was a great experience, as she would put on her apron and get right to it in that kitchen, showing me so patiently how to prepare several dishes, and after she saw that I had the confidence, she let me take over. She continued to order the food and determine what we ate each week, but the kitchen duties were mostly mine. I was so impressed and surprised to see her doing domestic type things like that. I was amazed that this lady, who was a math professor, could also roll up her sleeves and show me the ropes in the kitchen. I also learned that these highly educated and re-spected people enjoyed some of the same food that I did, but they just added a little more spice to it. I became a pretty good cook, and her apple pie recipe became one of my specialties, as it still is to this day.

It was a very pivotal time in the development of Virginia State's Mathematics and Science departments, and the Hunters were two of the key people involved, so they were extremely busy. As a result, there were times when both would be teaching classes, or in meetings simultane-ously, and since I was 19 years old when I started with them, I helped the Hunters with their daughter, Jean, who was eight years younger than me when I first moved in. Subsequently, I did not go out much and had plenty of time to study and do my class assignments. Jean was extremely bright, conscientious, and well behaved, so looking after her was easy for me. She was kind of quiet, and always seemed more mature than her age. An old soul is what she was, always engulfed in reading, studying, and her chores. Boy did she remind me of her mother. As they say, "the apple don't fall far from the tree," and that was so true with Dr. E. Louise Hunter and her daughter Jean. It was kind of like my mother and myself. I was the old soul amongst my siblings, very serious and responsible, just like Ma Macy Brown. I always liked when Mama talked to the other ladies in the neighborhood about how smart I was in school, and with doing my work and my chores. The big difference between Jean and me was that she never had to chop and stack wood, or work in the fields, or share a bed with a sibling like I had done throughout my childhood. She also never had to dream about what it would be like to have more because she always had it, but when I was her age, all I had was a dream.

Louise and John Hunter were both brilliant, ambitious, and very professional, but were very different as well. John Hunter was a charter member of the Alpha Phi Chapter of the Kappa Alpha Psi Fraternity, Inc. at Virginia State. He could be very funny, joking around often, and knew how to relax when the time was right. Louise was a proud member of the Alpha Kappa Alpha Sorority, Inc. (AKA). She was more serious-minded, even at home with the family. I noticed it after being there for only a few months, and I admired her for that. I figured it was not easy for a woman, especially a woman of color, to hold a position as a full-time professor, have a master's degree in mathematics, while pursuing her doctorate, and be respected and all. It seemed like she still had something to prove, and maybe she felt like she was carrying the weight of many other women on her shoulders. She probably wanted to be respected equally to the others in her profession, who were almost always men. That could be why she was not as laid back as John Hunter. He seemed to adore her, and very much respect her, though, and that was

43

very noticeable. I particularly remember him affectionately calling her "Lou-eyes" instead of Louise when he was in a playful mood.

They were both great mentors, and sometimes if he was helping me with something, he would always suggest that I get his wife's opinion about what we discussed. He genuinely admired her as a professional, and as his wife. They never seemed to compete with one another. They were a team, giving each other support and encouragement along the way. They were exceptional role models for me, and I watched them, took mental notes, and later modeled them often as a parent and spouse.

While living at the Hunter home, I had an opportunity to hear a lot about the value of being a member of a sorority since both were active members of their Greek-letter organizations. Louise Hunter was an Alpha Kappa Alpha (AKA) woman, and of course, her encouragement was a factor in me being interested in the Pink and Green for sure. I was really impressed to hear about the number of outstanding women who had joined and were active in the Sorority. I learned about networking and the importance of meeting other scholars and leaders like me. Mrs. Hunter made sure that I met some of these women on campus, which was all the motivation I needed to want to follow their paths and one day help others experience what I was experiencing, by seeing them as successful women and being of service to others. Just observing them, the way they spoke, and the classy way they carried themselves, was so impressive to me.

Before long, I was going through the usual pledging process of Greek organizations. My line sister Pearl and I were already connected because we were both math majors. I met some other wonderful ladies who were also pledging with me. We experienced the sometimes-difficult requests and mostly comical activities such as having to dress alike around campus and doing other odd things to please the "big sisters." I remember having to eat with my line sisters in the dining hall on campus, which I rarely did after moving in with the Hunters. The food was actually very good and was served family-style. It always smelled like Sunday afternoon in Ma Macy's kitchen when we stopped by for lunch at the big sisters' request. As pledgees, we had to pass the biscuits and gravy to the big sisters, and bless the table first, but it taught us the importance of serving and being dependable. Studying the amazing history of AKA together was very interesting as we learned about the founders of our Sorority, America's first Greek-letter organization for African American women. The secrecy of what was going to happen next each day was always a little nerve-racking, but we persevered and "crossed the burning sands." I was inducted into the Alpha Epsilon undergraduate chapter at Virginia State College. Our names were now etched into the illustrious history of AKA. Soror Pearl and I really bonded, as we were now "sisters" as well as women from similar backgrounds, with our eyes set on becoming leaders in the field of mathematics.

As was the case in high school, I also did not date much at all in college because I was too busy. I went to a few of my sorority events and activities, but my studying time was important to me, and so was my job with the Hunters. There were some girls who started dating too much and neglected their studies. Eventually, you didn't see them on campus, either because they flunked out or became pregnant. It's interesting how some of the girls who had babies never finished their education, but the guys who fathered the children always seemed to stay around and finish school and move on with their lives. I don't like to fail, so that was not going to be me. I made a commitment to myself to keep that scholarship and to graduate. Going back to the days of working on that farm was not an option.

My senior year came around so fast, and I was ready to move on and become a math teacher. I was doing well with my practice teaching, and I enjoyed working with the 7th-grade students I was assigned to. I had met my goal of graduating in four years, or so I thought. There was one last requirement that the seniors had to pass successfully to graduate. It was an English comprehensive exam that all students at Virginia State had to pass before graduation, and it was no joke. When I should have been excited about graduating, I was worried about not passing this test. A test that could possibly keep me from wearing that cap and gown and proving that I could achieve this goal that no one in my family had ever achieved. How would Ma Macy feel, and what would the Hunters say if I could not complete this last piece of the puzzle? Thankfully, I passed it on the first try. I was so happy because I heard that some students did not pass it and would not be allowed to graduate. I thought that test was going to be hard, but it wasn't that bad after all. For a moment, I felt bad for those who failed the test, but I could not help but feel proud of myself and relieved that I could now tell my family, my friends, and the Hunters that I would be graduating.

Graduation day was May 26, 1952, and it was the most exciting time my family and I had ever experienced since I could remember. It was an emotional experience as we passed by the Queen Anne styled Old President's House, and the historic Vawter Hall upon our arrival that morning. The campus sitting on that majestic hill above the Appomattox River, seemed more charming than ever that day, from its modest but dignified brick structures glistening in the sunlight, to the canopied, citrus fragranced magnolias that lined the hillside at what was the main entrance in those days, to the soft sounds of the college orchestra serenading the families and guests who were arriving for our big day. Those magnolias appeared to have grown at least a foot every year from the time I arrived as a freshman, and I couldn't help but reflect on just how much I had grown as a woman during those four years at State.

There were 338 graduates who would walk across the stage this day. The commencement speaker was Dr. Dwight O.W. Holmes, President Emeritus, Morgan State College (now University). My parents and siblings were there for the ceremony, as were the Hunters, who in their roles as faculty members were part of the procession. Their daughter Jean who was nearly fourteen at the time, sat with my family, right next to Ma Macy. I kept wondering to myself, "when is Mama going to pull her comb and brush out of her pocketbook and begin touching up that child's hair," but surprisingly, she left her alone. I guess she was so focused on her Gladys Mae walking across the stage that she didn't notice Jean's curls falling unmercifully to the heat and humidity that day.

This was certainly a day to remember, and one thing that especially stood out was the music. From the beginning of the ceremony, the selections during the program, starting with James Weldon Johnson's *Lift Every Voice and Sing*, filled me with a sense of pride and accomplishment I had never felt before, as I sat there among so many people of color, faculty, and graduates, who had succeeded against very difficult odds. Then there was the school alma mater and recessional at the end that also touched me so wonderfully.

The songs were so inspiring, uplifting, and gave me this upward push, and feeling that I must continue to rise and achieve more. It was emotional, yet I was confident, as I walked away prepared to serve and take on the world – Well, maybe not the world, but the Commonwealth of Virginia for sure. There is nothing like graduating from an HBCU, and lyrics like the following from the Virginia State Alma Mater still have a special place in my heart.

Forth we go to the world to do service

Thy lofty command to fulfill

With thy light go dispel all darkness

And thus, do thy Father's will.

Afterward, we all gathered at the Hunters' new place, as they had moved to a nicer home just off campus during my senior year. We celebrated with coca-colas, sandwiches, Ma Macy's country fried chicken, and Louise Hunter's amazing apple pie. The savory, pleasant smell of that chicken was taking me back in time to my childhood with our family in Sutherland, and I was thinking how blessed I was to have been raised by Nolan and Macy Brown. It was a "comfort" aroma that seemed to catch the attention of everyone that afternoon, even before Dr. Hunter blessed the table. It was a joy to see so many friends and family who came from Sutherland to join the celebration. On this day, I was the talk of the community. One of Butterwood School's own had gone beyond the rural boundaries of the tobacco fields and traveled another road. A path seldom taken by the women of my community, and whose only map or guide was the will to succeed. Certainly, Dorothy Bates had graduated and made us proud two years earlier, but this day belonged to me, and I enjoyed every minute of it. I was the first Brown to do it, and the first from my Mama's side of the family to finish college as well. It was a big accomplishment, but in my heart, I knew it was merely the beginning, the first step of many more to come.

After graduation, it was time to decide on my future, at least temporarily anyway. I didn't have money to go directly to graduate school, so I needed to find a job. I received a few teaching offers, but they were not in Dinwiddie County or Petersburg. The Hunters took me to interviews and helped me decide which job to take. I accepted a position at a segregated high school in Sussex County, Virginia, a very rural area in the Southeastern part of the State. The school was in the town of Waverly, where "Negroes" (or black folks), outnumbered the white population. I had no car and very little money, so with the help of the school principal, we found a lady who lived down the street from the school who kept teachers in her home, and I moved in with her. I didn't own very much at all at the time, so I packed up my trunk and a suitcase, which was a gift from the Hunters, and took the small, furnished room that would be my home for almost two years.

I came home most weekends, getting a ride from one of the other teachers, from the Hunters, or my Daddy. I taught eighth-grade math and science, so these were no babies, and it was a good experience for me. Not to my surprise, some of the kids were more worldly knowledgeable than me. It was in the deep country, and many of the families were sharecroppers or small farmers renting farmland, even more so than in Sutherland, so a lot of children were not in class when they were needed on their farms or at harvesting time. It was so challenging for the teachers there because quite often, when you thought you were reaching the students, they would be out of school for some time working, and you would have to start over with a new set of children.

I taught in Waverly, Virginia for two years, then with the concurrence of Louise Hunter, I decided to go back to Virginia State for graduate school. That teaching job did not pay much, but just like my Mama, I was very thrifty, and probably had the first dollar I made after I started working. I used some of the money that I had been saving to pay my tuition and room and board back on campus. I moved into Trinkle Hall, a familiar place, near my family, not far from the Hunters, and began working towards completing my master's degree in mathematics. I enjoyed eating at the campus dining hall, which served family-style, and the food seemed to be even better than before. Occasionally, I took in a meal with the Hunters as well. I completed everything in three semesters, one of those being a summer session. Graduation was May 30, 1955, and out of 255 graduates, there were 17 of us who had earned the Master of Science degree. So once again, I was looking for a job. A teaching offer came from Martinsville, Virginia, so I was on the road again, this time teaching high school math. Another step closer to what I wanted – to be the best mathematician I could possibly be.

My high school – The Dinwiddie Training School.

Vawter Hall is one of the more recognizable buildings at Virginia State.

My first home at Virginia State was the freshman women's dorm, Byrd Hall, pictured here in later years.

My Virginia State graduation portrait.

This is the high school where I taught mathematics after graduating from Virginia State. My first work job after college.

CHAPTER THREE: GOD'S BIG PLANS FOR ME

While I was teaching high school math in Martinsville, as wonderful as it was to give back to these children who were very much like me, I was sending job applications everywhere. I enjoyed teaching, and my parents were very proud of me, but I just kept thinking that there was something else that I was meant to do. The Supreme Court had recently reached a landmark decision on Brown vs. Board of Education of Topeka, Kansas, in which the court ruled that American state laws establishing racial segregation in public schools are unconstitutional, even if the segregated schools are otherwise equal in quality. Although the decision sparked reactions that ranged from elation to rage, this was undoubtedly a turning point in race relations in our country, but the schools in Virginia were still segregated and unequal since there was no ruling on when states had to integrate.

One month after the school year started, I received a letter from the Naval Proving Ground in Dahlgren, Virginia, stating that they were very interested in me. I had applied for a mathematician job there, and they wanted me to come to Dahlgren for an interview. The letter explained that they were about to take on some very important work and needed some good people in the math and science fields. It was exciting to receive that letter, but I still pondered over it for a few days. I wasn't sure if they were serious, and I couldn't find it on the map, so I had no idea where Dahlgren was located. It seemed like it was in the middle of nowhere, and I still did not have a car. How was I going to get there? More importantly, where would I live as segregation was still very much alive in Virginia. Maybe they did not know I was black, and when they saw my face at the interview, they would send me back home. After much thought, I turned down the interview, thinking I would just wait on something to come available in Petersburg or Richmond, or maybe the Washington, DC area because I had applied to jobs there as well.

Several days and weeks went by, and I did not hear from anyone else with a job offer or an interview for that matter. After a few weeks, I was wondering if I had made a mistake by not going on that interview, and then one day I heard back from the people in Dahlgren. I was selected for the job without an interview. They said there was a dormitory on the base that would be available for a small monthly fee, and the salary they were offering was twice what I was making as a teacher in Martinsville. This time there was not much to think about for a woman with a master's degree in mathematics, especially since no other offers were coming in. My only thought was if they were offering me a job in the United States government based solely on my qualifications, this must be God's plan for me. It wasn't long before I did the math and accepted the job. I notified the principal at Martinsville School that I was going to be leaving after only about 3 ½ months on the job, which was not easy to do, mainly because I would have to leave the students behind, but everyone there seemed to be very happy for me. It was perfect timing. I taught until the Christmas break and then spent a couple weeks with my family, getting prepared for my big move to Dahlgren in January of 1956.

When it was time to pack up and travel to Dahlgren, so many things were going through my mind. I was reflecting on the many experiences along the way that had enabled me to get to this point in my journey. I recalled things like the little one-room school on Butterwood Road, and being my class valedictorian in high school, earning a tuition scholarship to Virginia State, the children I had mentored while working as a teacher, and earning that first master's degree. All very important steps that were necessary, but none more impactful than the advice and mentoring I received while living with the Hunters. Finally, I was getting the mathematician job I had dreamed of, which was paying me more than twice as much as the teaching job I had just left. I had to accept it, even if it was in Dahlgren, a place that I had never heard of and could not initially find on the map. I would be going to a place where I knew no one, not even my supervisor, because I was never interviewed. Questions were swirling in my mind – How many black employees would be there, and would I be comfortable with this new work and living environment? Lastly, would I be smart enough to do the work they hired me to perform? All these questions came to mind because I was going to be a long way from that little farm in Sutherland, where I knew those tobacco fields like the back of my hand.

I felt like I had stepped up to another level professionally. It was the beginning of a career that I had been preparing years for and what I dreamed about for so long. It was truly a blessing, but I was still wondering if I was good enough. I was wondering if there would be others there who were from similar backgrounds as me. Others from small rural towns, segregated and unequal schools, and family backgrounds with little formal education. Things were starting to change gradually in America, so I was also going to be in a racially integrated environment for the first time. How would my co-workers react to me being there? What would it be like living on this Naval installation all by myself, in a dormitory with no other people who looked like me? All these thoughts were cluttering my mind. Nevertheless, I was excited.

On a cold but sunny Saturday morning in January, that early morning drive to Dahlgren allowed me time to reflect on all the growing up I had experienced over the years. I wondered if this was finally the road that I had dreamed of as a little girl, the one that would take me to the place far away from the woodsheds, barns, and tobacco fields that I was so familiar with. However, as I looked through the car window, it didn't appear that way, and the farther we traveled, the more things looked the same. My parents asked my younger brother Nolan Jr. to carry me to Dahlgren in his car. Although he had become very responsible by now, he didn't know where he was going any more than I did, but we had a nice new map that daddy had picked up from Olgers Store to help us find the way. Ma Macy said it would probably take a little better than two hours, so anticipating a long drive I dozed off to sleep for a short nap, then when I awakened and glanced at my watch, I realized we had been riding for over an hour and a half, so we were surely almost there. However, as I stared over my right shoulder, through the window, and into the countryside, it looked like we were still at home. I felt safe and comfortable, but this view was not the picture in my dream. It was not looking like those big city streets, with fancy homes and tall buildings that I had imagined. The view was still the same as before I took my nap, and this road to Dahlgren appeared to be just as country and remote as where I was coming from in Sutherland. As the late morning approached, there was nothing but farms and woods, and this narrow two-lane highway as far as I could see. Nolan Jr. seemed surprised as well, and I'm sure he was thinking the same as I was – *where in the world were we going? And why would the government have a naval base there?*

We continued to follow the directions on the map that called for an exit from Route 301 north, which should take us to our destination. Then I glanced up, and out of nowhere, I noticed some brick buildings through some trees on the right. We exited from the highway to a road that led us to a gate. There was a sign that read – Naval Proving Ground, Dahlgren, Virginia. I looked at Nolan Jr. and said, "This must be the place, little brother." He nodded in agreement. I had never been so happy than I was at that moment to see the entrance sign, nice sized buildings, and people inside the gate who looked like anything but farmers. Once we stopped at the gate, we had to announce who we were. I leaned over and gave the guard my driver's license and said, "I'm Gladys Mae Brown, sir, and this is my brother Nolan." The guard asked what I was there for, and I told him I was checking in to the dormitory and that I was starting my new job on Monday. He checked the list for my name and said, "Yes ma'am. Now, do you know where the dormitory is that you are reporting to Miss Brown?" I said that I didn't know where it was located. He pointed down the street and said, "It's that building right there. The building has two wings, one for women and one for men. There will be someone there to direct you to the women's side and check you in." It was right there, a stone's throw from the main gate. At least we would not get lost, I thought to myself. It was one of the brick buildings that we had noticed from the highway. I wondered why they told me I would have to rent an apartment at the women's dormitory, but now I knew. Outside of the base, there was nothing in Dahlgren, Virginia that I could see. They said over the phone that the rear of the base sat on the banks of the Potomac River, but it looked very doubtful at this point that a riverfront view from my apartment window was in my future.

By now, I was thinking a couple of things to myself. Could this be it, the beginning of that career and lifestyle that I had always imagined? Secondly, the guard, a white man, called me "ma'am," and I could not remember that ever happening before in my short life. This place did not have the appearance from outside the gate, but now that I was on the inside, I was starting to feel like this just might be the beginning of something special. After looking around at the buildings, the installation looked so official, and the more I looked, the more butterflies I felt inside. Nolan parked the car in the parking lot next to the building, and we proceeded to the entrance of the Dormitory. Despite being a little nervous, I stepped inside the door like I had been there before, with my little brother following me, struggling somewhat with my overpacked trunk, but he had carried heavier things than that back on the farm in Sutherland. I was determined to be strong and not look back. Forward was the only direction I knew when at home, and I didn't plan on changing now that I was in Dahlgren. There was no one at the front desk to assist me for some reason, but I didn't let it bother me. I just sat in the lobby with Nolan and waited, and I figured if I sat there long enough, somebody would realize I wasn't going anywhere and check me in. Eventually, the front desk clerk showed up, checked me in, and we headed to my room, ready to unpack.

I felt just as nervous this time as I did on my first day as a fresh-man at Virginia State, but I did not want anyone to know that, especially Nolan, Jr. He looked up to me, and I wanted him to know his big sister was going to be ok. Nolan and I hugged, I thanked him and assured him that I would be fine, and then he got in the car and drove back to Suther-land that afternoon. He had specific instructions from Ma Macy to get back home before dark because it still wasn't safe for a young black man to be traveling alone late at night in those days. Things were starting to change somewhat, but we were in the South – where the Ku Klux Klan, night riders, hate mongers and good ole boys were not dead by any means.

Here I was, all by myself, but I really was not afraid. It's mind-boggling to me now that I felt so secure back then. If that was to happen now, I would be very nervous. I think we were conditioned to be tough living on that farm, and besides, we had guards protecting us on this base and that was more than I ever had back home. It appeared that God must have had his hand in my life. I felt watched over, and I did not mind that we were in the country because I was from the country.

The first couple of days on the job were spent filling out paper-work with the folks in personnel and learning where the snack bar, cafe-teria, and bathrooms were located. I also sat down with a few of the other employees in my office to learn all of their functions and find out how things were generally done. I didn't know anything about the base be-cause we didn't have internet back then, so you couldn't just google something and find out about it. Also, this military base's mission was all about weaponry, and therefore everything was very secret, so if you didn't work inside the base you wouldn't really know what went on within those gates. I met with my supervisor, Mr. John Walker, on the first day. He worked for Mr. Ralph Niemann, the man who was head of the Department, and responsible for doing the hiring at the time. Mr. Walker took a lot of time with me since I did not go through the interview process, and he explained the history of the base. He explained that the base was named for Rear Admiral John A. Dahlgren, a U.S. Navy Civil War hero, who is considered one of the fathers of American naval weaponry. The facility was established on October 16, 1918, as a remote extension of the Indian Head Proving Ground, and was named the Lower Station, Dahlgren Naval Proving Ground when it first opened. The location on the Potomac River was specifically chosen for the development of a long ballistic range on the river, required for testing modern, high powered munitions. It became an extension of the Naval Research Lab in Washington, DC as well in the 1950s when satellite development was made a high priority. The National Aeronautics and Space Administration (NASA) had not yet been established.

I really liked how my supervisor took his time with me, explaining the history and the future expectations of our work. It was like we were going to change the way we looked at the world and outer space as well. It was exciting and made me feel like I was important, like I mattered. I was feeling all patriotic again, like I felt when I was in school back at Butterwood and we were going through WWII. He seemed confident that he had hired the right woman, but he did spend time asking me lots of questions to find out what I knew. I had earned bachelor's and master's degrees in mathematics and had been a high school teacher, but I was in a whole new world at Dahlgren, and he and I both knew it. After a brief tour of the facilities, it was quite clear: I was a long way from Butterwood Road.

Dahlgren was the primary site of U.S. naval computing, beginning with the 1948 installation of Howard Aiken's Mark II, followed by the Mark III in 1951. The center's next machine, the Naval Ordnance Research Calculator (NORC), was built at Columbia University's Watson Scientific Computing Laboratory. It was considered the first "supercomputer" (although not termed that at the time), and the most powerful computer on earth from 1954 to about 1963. Built by International Business Machines Corporation (IBM), it was delivered to Dahlgren in the Summer of 1955 and was the first time IBM used the term "computer" rather than "automatic calculator" or "data processing machine" to describe a stored program computing device. For a country girl like me, a huge computer like this was an amazing sight to see. It consisted of an Arithmetical unit, indicator panel, printers, and tape units. Nothing was spared in building this computer. As my supervisor explained, "It is extremely fast, very reliable, and yet with the simplicity of operation like never seen before." One of the top American engineers of that time, John Von Neumann, said it was, "the most advanced machine which was possible in that present state of art." This machine, the size of an entire room, was intimidating to say the least, but it was something I would have to get accustomed to working with over the next few years. A few months after I arrived, astronomer, Dr. Paul Herget said they used nine hours of running time and completed more computations than had ever before been done at one time in the history of astronomy.

This is a picture of the NORC, the supercomputer that was an amazing sight to see in 1956.

I wanted to adapt to this fascinating, new environment and succeed as soon as I could. I knew my work was cut out for me. As a double minority like I was, at a time where opportunities for women and people who looked like me were scarce, I felt there would be a lot of folks counting on me. There were other women of color who were coming behind me, the Hunters, and my family back home, and I absolutely wanted to make them proud. I met many of the employees those first few weeks, all of them white and mostly men. It was hard to remember names because there were so many people there and everything was happening so fast.

One thing I liked was the morning and evening break times. That is when we all gathered at the water coolers and the coffee makers for about 15 minutes. Most folks talked about the news of the day and about work assignments. I really concentrated more on names at break times, especially since it seemed they all knew my name. I was the only new kid on the block, I guess, so they only had to remember one name. It was a morning break time when I met Ira West, a young mathematician who was hired two months prior to my arrival and boy do I remember that day. He worked for Mr. Walker as well, but on a different team. I had initially noticed him my first day on the job. You could not miss him – there were only two black men in the building, other than the fellas who came in at night to clean up, empty the trash, and so forth. He seemed like a nice gentleman, sitting there in his chair, with perfect posture and big wide shoulders.

On my third day, he approached me during the morning coffee break. Ira pointed out later that I was dressed in my favorite blue pleated skirt and white blouse, a classic look during those times. As he poured his coffee and stirred in a spoonful of sugar, he didn't look quite so tall after all. He turned around to walk over to another group of guys, but out of the corner of my eye, I saw him pause then change direction as he headed back towards me. "Hello, I'm Ira West," he said. "You must be the new employee that we heard would be joining us. Welcome aboard." As I finished putting cream in my cup, I looked up in my usual business manner and quietly responded, "Hello Mr. West, I'm Gladys Brown." Our eyes met, almost as if it was destiny and Ira said with a warm smile, "It's a pleasure to meet you, Miss Brown," while extending his right arm for a handshake. I placed my cup on the table, shook his hand, and said, "It's nice to meet you, Mister, ahh." Recognizing quickly that I had forgotten his name already, he responded, "West, Ira West." I apologized saying, "I'm sorry, sir, remembering names has been the hardest thing to do around here. I never worked with so many people before," as I continued to be in business mode, despite feeling more comfortable with Ira than with the others. I thought he could be someone who could help me deal with the issues that might arise with me being a young black female in this recently integrated workplace. He seemed so confident for a black man in this environment. Then after sipping again from his coffee cup, he jokingly said, "Well, as far as I can see, there is no one in here that looks like me, so I should be easy to remember, right? Trying to keep it professional, I kind of chuckled and said, "Well, my break is almost finished, and I have to make a good impression in my first week, right, so I will talk to you later, sir." He politely responded, "Ok, and it's Ira West...don't forget now." I nodded shyly and walked away quickly so I would not have to answer, again keeping my space, but I thought to myself, *"this Ira West is a very nice young man"* – as I made sure not to glance back, thinking again *"my future at Dahlgren was looking up."*

The days and weeks quickly passed by it seemed, and I was getting more comfortable with my dormitory apartment, the nature of the work assignments, the functions of the office, and I was beginning to like more and more of what I was seeing in Ira. My dorm room was starting to feel like home. It was equipped with a double bed, a dresser, closet space, and plenty of room to move around. No television but I figured I could save and buy one in a year or two. Each floor had a kitchen, bathroom, and laundry room that we shared. The ladies on my floor were all white but they were courteous to me. Most of them spoke but did not have much to say, and we obviously were not trying to hang out in the evenings or anything like that. I did not expect anything more than just being cordial, though, because I knew this was new to them, and different for me as well. It was a little awkward using the bathrooms in the dorm and at the office building initially. When many of my white colleagues saw me in the bathroom, they would get this look on their face like they had seen a ghost or something. I was hardly that, but before my arrival, it wasn't every day they saw a black woman in the ladies' room. Over time, I got used to the looks from them, and they seemed to get more and more comfortable with little ole me. Some of them would even speak after a while. They might as well have because I wasn't going anywhere.

The only other black woman in the dorm was Clara. She lived one floor below me and was the first woman of color hired by Mr. Ralph Niemann. He was a good, honest man who felt strongly about integrating the workforce at Dahlgren and was one of the best managers that I ever met. He had great vision and foresight, bringing in those big computers, which required lots of mathematicians and scientists. Niemann believed that recruiting women and minorities into the workforce was one way to bring in people with very strong skills who may have been overlooked elsewhere. At a time when so many were overlooking those who looked like me, Niemann gave me a chance, the chance of a lifetime. I will always be grateful to him because of that.

One job I was particularly interested in was located at another Naval installation, the David Taylor Model Basin (DTMB), which later became one of the largest ship model basins-test facilities for the development of ship design in the world. It was the Carderock Division Headquarters of the Naval Surface Warfare Center and was built in 1938 in Bethesda, Maryland, near the Potomac River, a few miles northwest of Washington, DC. In recent times, it was named to the U.S. Register of Historic Places. I would have preferred to go there because of its proximity to DC. Sometimes things happen for a reason though, and when I look back, I know God's plan was for me to start my civil service career at Dahlgren. I later found out that some of my other black colleagues had applied to the David Taylor Model Basin as well, but no luck. I realized more and more that Niemann was ahead of his time, considering his progressive ideas on diversity, and how it could help improve a workforce situated in a remote geographical area like Dahlgren. He knew that recruiting would not be easy. Niemann hired Clara, Ira and a man named Herman Caster all by the end of 1955; and then me at the beginning of the new calendar year – January 1956. Clara had an engineering background and had taught at a high school in her native State of Missouri. I think she attended Lincoln University of Missouri, an HBCU in Jefferson City, but don't hold me to it. I never got to know her all that well because we worked on different projects, and by the time I arrived, she had met a man who lived off base in the black community in Dahlgren and would be off base with him a lot. When she was in the dormitory, she was quiet and often kept to herself.

A few weeks after I came on board, a young black woman from New York was hired and was supposed to work with us. She seemed to have a problem with the office she was assigned to, and she said she felt afraid being a black woman and living in the middle of nowhere, mostly because we were in the South, so the next night she stole out and went back home. We never saw her again. I suppose it was too far in the sticks for her. I always felt safe at Dahlgren. After all, it was a self-contained, high-security installation, with guards always on duty at the gate. There were no guards at the gate back at home. In fact, there was no gate there at all.

Of the four Black employees who were hired, Ira and I seemed to be interacting more than the others. There was something about him I liked, but I wasn't quite sure what it was yet. I do know that he was always helpful and especially in ways that only another black person could be. Ira was kind, respectful, and he must have had the patience of Job because initially, I did not hint at all that I was interested in him in any way other than professionally. I was happy to have a great friend already at the installation, which was something I had prayed for. Interestingly enough, I had been told by some guys back in Dinwiddie County that I should not accept a job in a place like Dahlgren because I would have a hard time meeting any eligible young black men there. I was glad I didn't pay that talk any mind though, because Ira West had some great qualities. He understood me when I just needed someone to talk to about the day to day issues of this new adventure of working in a newly integrated office situation not necessarily something that was comfortable or accepted by all involved. According to those naysayers, Ira was not supposed to be in Dahlgren, but he was, and he seemed to fancy me, and I was enjoying our friendship all the while.

Clara, the only other black professional woman, would escape the monotony and loneliness of the dormitory by leaving the installation confines often to be with her boyfriend, who was a blue-collar type who lived in the black community nearby. Herman was already married and lived in an apartment for couples on base with his wife, so he also had someone to confide in after hours. Ira and I were communicating, but he says I kept the conversations about business and general topics, and never gave him any hint that I was interested in him on a personal level. I thought he was a nice man and colleague, but that was it. It had become apparent that he was attracted to me, and I was flattered, but I always believed in taking my time to get to know a person before dating and so forth; I wasn't going anywhere and neither was he, so no need to rush, and besides, I am sure all eyes were on us in that first year of them hiring black professionals, so we had to always stay in business mode and make a good impression. We were just as serious about our work as the other folks, but we had more at stake and more to prove, being the first black professionals hired at Dahlgren; we wanted and needed our work ethic to be obvious.

The work was interesting; I was learning to code and program that big computer, along with all the other mathematicians on the staff. As Ira says, I was all business those first few months, so we would only see each other during break times, and I would see him at the chapel on base on Sundays and chat a bit after church. Some weekends I would ride home on the Greyhound Bus to spend time with my family. Ira did not have a car the first few months that I was in Dahlgren, so he would catch the same bus because it would stop in Richmond, Virginia, which was his hometown. He would get off there and I would continue riding to Petersburg. My Daddy or Nolan, Jr. would pick me up from there. We were so isolated in Dahlgren, so our best means of transportation was to take a bus to get back home or catch a ride with someone who had a car. Ira was from Richmond and he was just as poor as I was, so he was saving for a car. I was saving too, but remember, I was from the country, so it was fine with me not to have a car. I was more intent on giving back to my family.

The house my parents bought with the help of Mr. Olgers in North Dinwiddie.

I was helping my parents with their payments on the new house they had built with the help of Mr. Olgers, the owner of the general store in Sutherland. The house, which had a little more space, was nothing fancy, but clearly a step up from the house that I grew up in. My parents could not have done it without Mr. Olgers, who loaned them the money to purchase the land and build the house. The banks were rarely giving loans like this to black folks, so Daddy was fortunate that he had established a friendship over the years with Olgers. I initially started helping them pay back some of the money to Olgers after they finished building the house about a year after I began teaching. I always felt that I should help them for all they had done for me.

This is me during my early days at Dahlgren.

Some of my first assignments involved computing range tables for weapons systems, which was first in line with the traditional ordnance development role of the facility. I was assigned to work with a white lady who was there before me. We got along well, although not much was said in the beginning. We just did our work, stayed cordial, then once we got to know each other and respect each other professionally, we became friends. She and I worked on that huge computer and on the Marchant calculators together for several months. I remember hearing the firing of the guns and weapons from the range as they were testing weapons constantly, and pictures on the wall would start rattling. We became accustomed to it though since this became quite regular at certain times of the day. As time passed, new missions were on the horizon. Ira worked in the area that dealt with submarine launched ballistic missiles. We came to Dahlgren at the start of the satellite era, so things were changing for me and Ira, as well as for America and the rest of the world. We were leading the world in science, technology, and military power. There was some debate about whether satellite launching projects were practical or more necessary than developing ballistic missiles with an imperative need to prevent a strike against the United States by the Soviet Union. The consensus was that we should concentrate on security requirements first, and assign the Vanguard satellite program as secondary, but still important in the race against the Soviet Union's satellite ambitions. Our mission, therefore, was to speed up the development of intercontinental ballistic missiles with enough retaliatory power to discourage attack. The security of our nation and civilization, it was thought at that time, would depend on our ability to shoot across the ocean quickly and accurately before the Soviet Union had missiles available that could shoot at us.

The Dahlgren Laboratory played a big part in this, since we were a remote post of the Naval Research Laboratory in Washington, DC, which was more focused on scientific endeavors for the government than it was for armed forces work. Large numbers of scientists, engineers and other brilliant people were filling up the hallways at Dahlgren and coming up with all kinds of algorithms, and we had to do the work to compute this data.

I was going home most weekends and couldn't say too much about my work assignments to the family, but my parents were very proud of me. I think my daddy stuck his chest out a lot more whenever he had to make a stop at Olgers Store. He may have even come up with more reasons to visit the store just so he could drop by and brag on me. Ma Macy was surely reminding the church sisters that her Gladys Mae was now a mathematician, working for the government. Sometimes I took the bus, and sometimes I would ride with the lady that I was assigned to who had become a good friend. She was white and older than me, but we somehow got past the racial barriers that were so prevalent then and got to know each other. Her name was Thelma, and she was from North Carolina. She had a car and would let me drive all the way to Petersburg, and then she would drive the rest of the way to her home in North Carolina. Those long rides with Thelma helped me realize that we are all basically the same, no matter what color, if we get to know a person's heart and soul, not just observe the color of their skin. I realized that she was better than most, and it was good to have a female friend to share things with that only another woman working in that male dominated environment in the 1950s would understand. We took those weekend trips home several times until Ira bought a car about 3 months after I met him. That 1953 Chevrolet was a game changer, as Ira would say.

Did I mention that I was dating another man at the time that I was hired to work at Dahlgren? Well, I was, and that was another reason I was keeping it professional with Ira. There was a guy back home who I had met at Virginia State. He was teaching somewhere near Richmond, so we had not gone out often, but he was the guy who would pick me up when I would get off the Greyhound bus at the Richmond Bus Station.

He carried me home to Sutherland several times. Ira didn't know for sure, but he kind of figured it out. I think Ira bought that car a little sooner than he wanted to so he could take me home to Sutherland himself. I believe he thought I would give him a chance if he had a car. I was still not sure about being more than friends with Ira, so when he offered to give me a ride to Sutherland, I asked him to drop me off at the Richmond Bus Station, and I would get home from there.

One week, about five months after we met, I decided that I wanted Ira to meet my parents, so I called Ma Macy and told her that I wanted her and my Daddy to meet Ira. She had heard me speak about him before and thought it was a good idea. I was starting to really like Ira, and I had long stopped seeing the other fellow. I knew that if my mother liked Ira then he was probably the man that God had placed in my life. Ira was to carry me to Richmond like always, but before we drove off, I asked him if he could take me the rest of the way to Sutherland and meet my family. He seemed so happy but not real surprised. It was as if he knew it was coming. We arrived at the house and Ira was as impressive as always. Before I knew anything, he and Ma Macy had hit it off. Ira enjoyed the country setting, being from the city and all. He and my daddy talked about farming. The rest of my family seemed to like him as well. Ma Macy thought he was a perfect gentleman, and he said she was the nicest woman he had ever met other than me, of course. That day was when I knew we were special together, and that I wanted to take the relationship beyond just a workplace friendship. Ira says he had already decided that I was the one soon after he saw me in that blue pleated skirt and white blouse while at coffee break, despite me not remembering his name. He drove to Richmond to stay with his mother that night and then returned to pick me up the next day. There would be many more rides with Mr. Ira West, but as we drove back from Sutherland this first time, I looked over at him a few times and realized how blessed I was to have the right man for me at this pivotal time in my life. I gave him a great big hug when he pulled up outside the women's dorm at Dahlgren, the first of many.

As things happen, we were "courting" now, and our friendship grew into a great relationship. As we leaned on each other and helped each other through the remainder of this first year at Dahlgren, I couldn't help but think to myself – *What would I do without Ira's friendship, advice, comforting, and love?* It was not easy being such a small minority in this place far away from the farm, with weapons being tested all day, and a computer as big as the house I grew up in. Ira was a great partner, and I was the same for him. We ate lunch together often, went to chapel together, and took walks on the base. Ira had started playing on one of the office softball teams that summer, and boy was he good. All eyes were on Ira when he was at bat, and he looked so cute out there wearing his Brooklyn Dodgers baseball cap. The Dodgers had won the World Series the year before, with his favorite player Jackie Robinson leading the way. Ira had played baseball all his life and was a natural at 3rd base for his Army installation team overseas, where he made such an impression that he was invited to play with a Cincinnati Reds minor league team when he returned from the Korean conflict. However, he returned to Virginia Union in Richmond, Virginia, the school he attended before he joined the Army. He wanted to go back to school and make a better life for himself. He got his degree in mathematics, while cutting hair on the side. He had learned his barbering skills while a student at Maggie

Walker High School in Richmond. He was a very good barber and was cutting hair in the neighborhood even as a teenager. Not long after receiving his degree, he was hired at Dahlgren. Ira felt that his experience in the military was a key factor in being considered for the job at Dahlgren. He played baseball with the white guys in the military, which showed his ability to work well with them, and became the second black male that Niemann hired. He was sort of the "Jackie Robinson" type that they were looking for, level-headed, even-tempered, and one who wouldn't have a problem working alongside white folks.

We were not going home as often now, so we tried to find businesses in the black community of Dahlgren that we could patronize. We did not mingle too much with the people in the community. However, our favorite place to have fun was the Blue Note, only a couple miles down the road. It was a restaurant that doubled as a club after hours. We could dance to the music of the jukebox and relax with folks who looked like us. We liked to go on Wednesday evenings since that was the day it never got very crowded, and secondly, it was not the safest place to be on weekends, if you know what I mean. We would eat a little something, dance to the sounds of some music by Nat King Cole and other artists of the time and relax there for a while. We really enjoyed ourselves. Then it was back to the base to get some rest since we both had early hours. We were the only "professional" types that seemed to patronize the Blue Note, except when Herman Caster and his wife would drop in. Most of the customers there liked us and kind of looked at us with pride because of our positions on the naval installation. The patrons were from the surrounding area, mostly farmers, housekeepers, and service industry workers. Quite often, when we were at the Blue Note, we saw many of the janitors, trash collectors, and laborers who worked on the base. It was also where I met my hairdresser that I kept for nearly 50 years. We also met a guy there named Charles Garland, who became our tailor for years. He was a great dancer, and one of the folks in the community that really liked and respected us. He told Ira that it made him feel proud to see folks that looked like him working in professional roles at Dahlgren.

We began to spend most of our free time together. Going to movies, shopping, and eating meals together. People knew if they saw one of us, the other was not far behind. Our friendship had quickly grown into much more, and after just over a year at Dahlgren, we began to talk about spending the rest of our lives together. It was the next thing to do in a relationship like ours back in the day. Ira made it known that I was everything he wanted in a woman, and quite frankly, I couldn't think of a better man to share my life with. There was a woman from my church in Sutherland who would say to the young girls, "Don't bother with trash…because trash gets in your eyes." That's how she referred to men who were not worthy of a good woman. Clearly, Ira West was not that type of man. We were best friends and shared so many goals, interests, professional and spiritual values. I looked at how he treated his wonderful mother with so much love, honor, and respect, and I was sold. He supported me as a woman with strong professional desires and ambitions, respected my family and enjoyed listening to me talk about my farm girl background. I was a country girl, and Ira was a city guy, but he always seemed to understand my "country."

Folks considered you an old maid back then if you came out of school and you didn't have a steady boyfriend and no intentions of marriage. Neighbors and family alike always told me since I was in college,

I needed to find a nice young man to settle down with and start a family. However, I felt that I needed to be able to take care of myself. It was said that a woman should get married and the man will take care of her, but at times the man disappears or walks away – and then you must start all over again. Sometimes I felt like an old lady when I heard that kind of old maid talk because I still strived to take care of myself and laid out my plans about how I could do it without a man. Then along came Ira, and I just knew he was the one. Besides, Ma Macy thought he suited me.

It seemed that everything fit with Ira and I, like a completed puzzle. In March 1957, we decided to get married, but it was not a big production. I was a relatively private person, and so was the engagement period. There was no big proposal and no special night out. We just knew our hearts and minds were telling us it was time. We started planning, but there was not much to plan. We went shopping around for an engagement ring in Richmond. We didn't know much about wedding rings, so we did some studying and decided it was a diamond solitaire that we liked. Both of us wanted to get a good buy for the money, so we started looking for a good clear diamond, and finally, we were successful. I received the ring one weekend, and first things first, we wanted to announce our intentions to our parents. Ira said he would go with me to tell my daddy and Ma Macy in person…and ask for Daddy's approval. Ira was just so respectful like that. He didn't have a father in his life, but his mother was a wonderful parent and had instilled so many values in Ira and his brother Roy. Everything went well, and toward the end of our visit, Ma Macy said we could have the ceremony at the house and save a lot of money. She said it was more important we were marrying the right person for all the right reasons than to have a big expensive wedding. Daddy and Ira excused themselves and walked outside and talked for quite a while. I'm not sure what they discussed that day, but I can say that the two of them became the best of buddies after that. Whenever you saw them, they would be laughing and joking, and talking sports and men stuff I reckon. We stopped in Richmond on the way back to Dahlgren to share the news with Ira's mother, Blanche Estelle West. She was happy for us as well and urged Ira to be a good husband. He told me later that she always told him that she was proud of him for choosing a good woman to be his bride. That Monday, after returning to Dahlgren, we announced our engagement at work.

The wedding was held at my parent's house in Sutherland on June 15, 1957. To say it was a small ceremony would probably be an overstatement, so if you're expecting lots of glamour, frills, and trimmings, then you could probably skip to the next paragraph. The wedding party consisted of my sister Annie, who was the Maid of Honor, and Ira's brother, Roy was his Best Man – that was it. There were no designated wedding colors, so any color worked that day. I wore a short, white, sleeveless wedding dress with a drop waistline, and lines of stitching across the bodice. My head piece was a fingertip veil. I was no farm girl on that day if I must say so myself. Ira was so handsome that day in his white tuxedo jacket and black trousers. We did not have much in the way of decorations. Nothing flashy, just a few flowers, and the food was cooked by one of the Virginia State employees that I had known from my graduate school days on campus. He was a country gentleman who was good at decorating cakes and doing food for groups, but again nothing fancy compared to most weddings of today. My brothers said the cake was delicious, but I don't remember because, you know, I was the bride and had to greet and mingle most of the day. Ma Macy advised us not to go in debt on your wedding day, and we stayed true to that. We did not spend a lot of money, but we have fond and sentimental memories of our June wedding, of us coming together as one, and exchanging our vows, witnessed by a small gathering of family and good friends. It was simple yet romantic, our special day.

Now those of you who were looking for glamour and frills may come back and join me. After the vows were said and done, and a half-day of celebration with our loved ones, Ira and I were Mr. and Mrs. West; and next to come in this great adventure that only God could have planned was our honeymoon. We did it up big this time… well, kind of. The night of the wedding, we stayed in Richmond with Ira's brother Roy. The next morning, we drove to the Richmond Station to catch a train to Atlantic City, New Jersey. It was actually a very popular romantic destination at that time, with casinos, nice restaurants, night life and all. We spent our unforgettable honeymoon walking the boardwalk, sampling good food, enjoying the beach, and relaxing in our guest room of course. After a few fun and sun-filled days by the sea, it was back to work at Dahlgren for both of us. It felt good that we did not overspend on that wedding and still had money in our pockets to start out on this life adventure – thanks to the man upstairs and the good sense we had learned from Daddy, Ma Macy and Ira's mom, Blanche. And by the way, sixty-three years later, I still wake up with the man who put my family and me above himself, and I continue to wear and cherish that diamond solitaire ring.

Wedding Day and cutting the cake. It was held in the country at Ma Macy's house.

An aerial view of the Dahlgren Base situated on the Potomac River.

(Below) At Dahlgren, behind the Dormitory, walking to the Office.

CHAPTER IV. BOOMTOWN

There were many congratulatory well wishes and cards awaiting us when we returned to work at Dahlgren after our wedding and honeymoon. Most of the co-workers at Dahlgren were not surprised when we announced our wedding plans. Some of them had gifts for us, and a few of them expressed, in private, that they had expected us to get married sooner than we did. We had become that kind of couple, I guess – when you see one of us, the other must not be far behind. Now we were living together in one of the many six-unit housing structures designed specifically for families who needed housing on the base. No more dormitory rooms. We were now residing in the section of the base called Boomtown.

Dahlgren was officially established in 1918 as a Naval Proving Ground. Prior to that, the Navy operated a proving ground at Indian Head, Maryland, but advances in gun designs and ordinance made its range obsolete. The range was required to be over water, and the area from Machodoc Creek and Point Lookout on the Potomac River was selected because of its straight lines and accessibility. The climate and relative calm of the river were also factors. At the time of Dahlgren's

85

establishment, the area was extremely remote and unpopulated. It was in the middle of nowhere. Recruiting and retaining the highly specialized workforce required that the Navy promise to supply housing, food, medical services, schools, recreation, and other socially needed infrastructure. In the 1950s, as the Dahlgren installation began to hire more Black employees, there was an even more dire need to provide housing on the base because of segregation and restricted covenants that denied renting and selling homes to blacks in the housing industry at that time in Virginia.

Boomtown and Tarrytown were the two communities located on the base. Tarrytown, consisting mostly of single-family homes, required that you were a longer-tenured worker or higher-level employee. Otherwise, you had to wait your turn for a unit. We were not, therefore, we lived in Boomtown those first years of the marriage. It was like any other neighborhood with people living in close-proximity, big families, and some couples, who were just starting out like Ira and me. One person in the household, usually a male, worked on the base in some capacity. There were some women who were mathematicians or science professionals, who also qualified for base housing above the dormitory level if they were married and had a family. There was the Dahlgren School located on the base that went from kindergarten through eighth grade. Children had to enroll at a school off base once they reached ninth grade, where they attended King George High School about 12 minutes away. The Dahlgren Chapel, where Ira and I would meet each other on Sundays when we first met, was also located in the community. It was the mid-1950s, so obviously most of the residents were white, and that was something that we had to adjust to, as well as them adjusting to living with us.

Now how did all this growth occur necessitating more housing at this Naval facility in the remote Northern Neck area of Virginia? Prior to World War II, the Dahlgren installation devoted most of its attention to proof firing new guns and heavy weapons that were manufactured at the naval gun factory in Washington, then shipped down the Potomac to Dahlgren by barge, and then test fired to establish the gunnery tables. Workers also performed limited experiments with new weapons and equipment. Then research and development programs were improved at the installation during war time. Dahlgren began new laboratories during World War II, beginning with an armor and projectile laboratory in 1941. During that decade, it expanded its laboratory work to include the studies of gauges and measurements, aviation ordnance, rocketry, and trajectory calculations. The trajectory calculations resulted in the use of new electronic calculating machines that were the precursors of modern computers, which is important because eventually mathematicians would be needed, and the base personnel would continue to grow, and did it ever by the time we started our careers.

Looking back, Boomtown may have got its name because it was where the middle-income employees, military and civilian, lived with their families. Remember, it was the time period when the "baby boomers" were being born, and maybe someone had the clever idea of naming this section of base housing after the baby boomer phenomenon, which was big in America at the time. However, I read an article by Cathy Dyson, of The Free Lance-Star in Fredericksburg a few years ago about longtime Dahlgren resident Thomas Mason, who was there when the residences were built. He was born on a farm just outside the base two years after its establishment in 1918. The land that he grew up on had been purchased by Mason's father from a Civil War veteran who used to wear his gray uniform to church sometime when Mason was a young boy. According to Mason, the name "Boomtown" was given to the residential area because of the rapid growth in new employees entering the work-force at Dahlgren between 1941 and 1945, the World War II years. Mason and his wife were among the first to live in the homes while he worked there in the early 1940s. Neatly lined up in rows, there were more than 130 new apartments, single-family homes, and duplexes, modestly built, to meet the need of the large influx of newcomers, and aptly named Boomtown. Either way, the name given to the base community was fitting, and it turned out to be our home, and the home of many of our friends for several years, with many lasting memories.

Viewing our building or duplex from the main entrance – there was a one-story single unit on the left. Then there were two stacked units, side by side, one unit on top of the other. There was another one-story unit on the right, opposite the other one-story unit. We lived on the ground level in the one-story unit on the left of the entrance. Each family had the responsibility of keeping their section or unit of the building looking livable (window treatments, furniture, etc.). We had pretty good neighbors, so it was a nice experience overall. We agreed that this would be a nice place to start a family, on a military base, with good activities, a nice school, and a wonderful Chapel that you could walk to on Sundays. Naturally, as most newlyweds did at that time, we started working on increasing our family size soon after we settled into Boomtown.

There was so much going on in the world regarding the development of missiles, satellites, and eventual space travel, and we seemed to be right in the middle of it as Dahlgren employees. The United States had been anticipating that the Soviet Union would try to put an artificial satellite into orbit, and on October 4, 1957, they did it. Sputnik 1 orbited for three weeks before its batteries died, and the satellite fell back into the Earth's atmosphere. Scientists began tracking and studying Sputnik 1 from Earth, which provided valuable information. The Soviet Union sent Sputnik II into orbit soon after, and the space race had begun. On January 31, 1958, Explorer I was the first satellite launched by the United States, following the Sputnik I and Sputnik II launchings. This was the beginning of the Cold War Space Race between our nation and the Soviet Union. It was ground-breaking news and a historic moment, and even more important to us at Dahlgren. The Cold War placed more demands on us to develop new offensive and defensive ship systems. The Naval Space Surveillance Center also moved onto the base because of our growing computer advances, and we became more involved in developing Fleet Ballistic Missiles, which we later called Submarine-Launched Ballistic Missiles. So only a few months after our wedding, the honeymoon was figuratively and literally over. We were both required to get Top-secret clearance and were informed the work was not to be discussed outside of our Dahlgren facilities.

This was the time period before the National Aeronautics and Space Administration (NASA), so the U.S. Ballistic Missile Agency was directed to launch the Explorer I satellite, which made its final transmission of data in May of 1958, and several other Explorer attempts later were not as successful. The Naval Research Laboratory (NRL), which had been involved in the satellite development since 1955, initially conducted the first American satellite program called Vanguard. The program was initiated to represent the United States in the International

Geophysical Year (IGY). IGY was a cooperative international scientific effort to study the physical properties of Earth. A competition was held to determine which US government agency would build and launch the satellite. NRL had to design, build, launch, place in Earth orbit, and track an artificial satellite carrying a scientific experiment. NRL then constructed the first complete satellite launching facility at Cape Canaveral, Florida. The Vanguard I satellite was successfully launched into Earth's orbit on March 17, 1958. The Vanguard I satellite achieved the highest altitude of any man-made vehicle at that time, and established, beyond doubt, geologists' suspicions that Earth is pear-shaped. Interestingly enough, Vanguard I orbits the Earth today as the oldest man-made satellite and will remain in orbit well into the 22nd century. As you can see, the Navy played a major role in the space race in the first years of my career.

There were more black professionals employed at Dahlgren now, and most of them lived in Boomtown. The others who arrived there along with us, such as Herman Caster and Clara Scranage, were there with their families, and several other black mathematicians had been hired in the months after we came on board. The Jones family, that I had not mentioned to this point, came to Dahlgren in the Spring of 1956 and were also our neighbors. Orbie Jones, Sr. was another one of Niemann's hires as a mathematician. He was from Missouri and was an HBCU graduate of Lincoln University of Missouri, with a B.S. degree in Mathematics. He had been working as a high school math teacher and decided to take Niemann's offer at Dahlgren. He and his wife Azellar had two young children at the time.

There was always a need to keep balance in our lives, so we socialized with some people that we knew and respected from the office. The men, black and white, enjoyed playing basketball, softball, and football on weekend afternoons, and seemed more comfortable with each other a lot sooner than the women since they were spending time with each other outside of the office. There was also a little league team that was started on base, and many of the fathers were involved in coaching as well. The black women had a harder time getting to know the white women of Boomtown because there were no activities to participate in with them, such as sports. Subsequently, we formed a social group that, now that I look back, was segregated. Only black women were members of this club. We never said the white women could not join, but we also never invited them in either. We had meetings and hosted parties. There were birthday celebrations and holiday get-togethers for our families and children also. These gatherings were fun and a great way to release some of the tension that would build up during the week. There was discrimination and difficult experiences all around us, on and off the base, so our time together gave us a chance to bond and vent a little as well.

The club members even had an opportunity to discuss the events going on that were affecting our people, such as the Little Rock Nine, the group of black students that were the first to integrate the schools in Little Rock, Arkansas in 1957. The Arkansas Governor called in the Arkansas National Guard to block the students from entering the building. Then about 3 or 4 weeks later, President Dwight D. Eisenhower sent in federal troops to escort the Little Rock Nine into the school. I remember we all saw those pictures from a copy of Ebony magazine, and not one of us had a dry eye. Our tears of joy and mixed emotions summed it all up. We also found out about the Southern Christian Leadership Conference being formed and about its new Chairman, Dr. Martin Luther King, Jr., by sharing the articles from the Ebony magazine each month. That was the way black folks got information back then, along with black churches, or in school. There was never much information about us in local newspapers back then unless it was something negative.

Things were happening all the time when it came to our civil rights, and we were aware that we were witnessing history. Desegregation was a hot topic, but our white co-workers never brought it up. It seemed that they didn't know anything about what was going on outside those Dahlgren gates. Or maybe they thought it would just go away, but it didn't. Virginia was one of the States whose Senators and House members had signed the Southern Manifesto, opposing integration of schools, after the U.S. Supreme Court ruled that integration must occur "with all deliberate speed" in Brown vs. Board of Education II. The Virginia Governor, J. Lindsay Almond, threatened to shut down any school if it was forced to integrate. He did just that, first in Front Royal, then two more schools in Charlottesville, and six schools in Norfolk, Virginia. It was good that we had each other to talk to through these turbulent times, and it was a blessing to have Ebony Magazine bringing us the news of Black America. The civil rights movement was very much active by now, and we could only wonder what would happen next. We continuously made sure to work twice as hard as our white counterparts.

We continued to go out to the Blue Note on Wednesdays for some good soul food that was as close to home cooking as one could get in Dahlgren. It was also a chance to let off some steam from the continuous heavy workload of our jobs. However, most evenings I cooked for the two of us. I enjoyed cooking and was a pretty good cook. I had cooked for the family while growing up at home, giving Ma Macy a break at times. I also had a lot of experience cooking for the Hunters while working for them as an undergraduate at Virginia State. When I was cooking, it was always an opportunity to create my own special dishes, and I enjoyed seeing people smile when eating food that I prepared. That was probably something I picked up from watching Ma Macy when I was a kid. I also had enough common sense to know that if Ira could eat that food he was served in the Army, then he surely could eat my cooking, which I had mastered down to a science. A little bit of Ma Macy's country, a few parts Dr. Hunter's spices, and of course, being math-minded and very organized, I had a knack for precisely mixing and measuring ingredients. So with that combination, and "putting my foot in it," if you will, Ira smiled a lot that first year, and put on a few pounds as well.

It was 1959, the year Alaska and Hawaii were the last states admitted to the Union. Hard to imagine now…seems like they've always been there – Lorraine Hansberry's A Raisin In The Sun opened on Broadway with a young Sidney Poitier – The United States had earlier recognized the new Cuban government of Fidel Castro, and President Eisenhower met with Soviet Union Premier, Nakita Khrushchev on U.S. soil. As time went by, my body was feeling different, like something I had not felt before. Well, just as I thought, I was expecting. I will never forget telling Ira and seeing that smile on his face. We were going to have a child, and excited was an understatement for how we were feeling. We regularly took those weekend drives to the country to see the family and enjoy being away from the office. Not having to hear those vibrating noises of the guns being tested every day at the proving ground ranges was also a benefit of getting away also. I always enjoyed the ride over to Sutherland, relaxing with the windows open and taking in the sunlight and breath of fresh air, while Ira did all the driving, of course. On our way, we sometimes stopped to get gas at the filling station or had to stop at a traffic light in town. I remember it was starting to feel a little strange to see the "White Only" signs still in public places. After all, we were now working and living in an integrated environment, but once we stepped off the grounds, it was still a segregated South that our brothers, sisters, and parents were subjected to. Even with our government jobs and credentials, it was the same for us as well, and maybe even worse because Ira and I were better off now than most of the white folks in those parts. Back when I was living under those Jim Crow laws, it never affected me that way because that's all I knew, but now that I was living inside the gates of the Naval Base, it seemed so much more degrading to see those signs. Not to mention, I was pregnant now and would have to bring a child into a world with so much hate.

Ma Macy, Daddy, and my siblings and friends in Sutherland were so happy to hear that we were expecting, and always pampered me when we visited. They wouldn't even let me pick vegetables from the garden as I normally did when I had visited before. Ma Macy announced that only Ira had permission to pick those fresh beans, collards, and tomatoes, with a little help from my brothers, Joseph, Nolan, Jr., and Joseph's daughter, Jackie, who was just barely school age. My sister Annie was living in Lynchburg, Virginia by this time. She moved there after she graduated from St. Paul's College, an HBCU in Lawrenceville, Virginia, and was teaching home economics at a school in Nelson County. Joseph lived across the street, had served in the Korean War, and was married to a Dinwiddie County girl that he had known in school. Nolan, Jr. was living down the road a bit from Daddy and Ma Macy. They all routinely helped Ma Macy and Dad with the farming and the garden work. Jackie's sister, Francine, was still too young to help them out, so she would sit beside me or in my lap and give me hugs when she wasn't attending to a younger sibling. Ira was becoming pretty good working out in the garden, for a city boy from Richmond. He was almost a natural. I just sat back and watched and gave a few instructions every now and then, but boy did they pamper me, and I enjoyed every minute of it. The peace and quiet, and love that I got from my family was always worth the trip to Ma Macy's.

One day while working at the office at Dahlgren, the unthinkable occurred. I received a phone call from my brother, informing me that my father had died. It was a shock as he was only 52 years old. The man that I had looked to as an example of how a man should treat a woman and raise his children had suffered a fatal stroke at home and was suddenly gone from our lives. As soon as Ira and I could get away from the office, we were on our way to see about Ma Macy. That two-hour drive to Sutherland seemed like forever, and all I could think about was, *What do I say to Ma Macy when I see her?* I was still in my twenties, so losing loved ones was new to me. Once we arrived, there were very few words. I comforted my mama, and she comforted me, while we cried together and wiped the tears from each other's faces. There were no words that could explain how we felt any more than that picture of us at that moment standing together, with the garden and fields that daddy tended so meticulously, surrounding us in a metaphorical kind of way – almost as if he was wrapping his arms around us. It was time to be strong for Mama and help her get through this difficult time.

I couldn't stop thinking about how he was so happy seeing me just a week earlier, and how he was so elated about my pregnancy. My daddy, who always consoled and encouraged me to be strong and persevere through any adversity, had gone. He learned how to get through tough times from his mother, Grandma Plum, who I never saw shed a tear or get emotional about anything. The mental toughness I had always admired from that side of the family, had somehow escaped me, and Daddy was not there to guide me and give me strength like he always did before. We were all grieving and in a state of disbelief, but I knew Ma Macy was feeling more than we were. It must have been devastating for her to lose her husband at a relatively young age, knowing she would have to carry on without him. Grandma Plum must have had a very hard time as well, as no parent wants their children to go before them, not even a strong woman like her. When I look back to the day after my daddy had gone too soon, I think that was a turning point for me. It is when I started to become the resilient, strong Gladys...and thank goodness because I would need it. My life, with all its ups and downs, was just getting started. This is when I realized that I was to be a leader in this family, and I accepted the challenge like Daddy would have wanted me to. I helped Ma Macy with the funeral arrangements and kept her spirits up, with Ira's help, of course, as he was there for both of us. Ira was strong like Daddy, and times like this reassured me that I had chosen the right man to be my life partner.

There was an outpouring of love and kindness from the community. The church was packed for my daddy's going home service, with family and friends, and some people I didn't really know well, but they sure seemed to love and respect Nolan Brown, Sr., and that meant a lot to Ma Macy, my siblings and me. They all told me how proud he seemed when he talked about his Gladys Mae being a mathematician for the Navy. There was a lot of spirit in that old church, and several folks got up and testified about how Daddy had helped them out in some way. Even Mr. Olgers, the store owner, came to the service that day, as well as a few other white folks in the area, and that didn't usually happen in Sutherland. It was hard leaving Ma Macy there without Daddy when Ira and I had to return to Dahlgren. Before we got on the road, I hugged her firmly and told her we would always be there for her; that's something I committed myself to. Weekends, holidays, and family reunions with Ma Macy would become an even bigger part of my life now, with Ira always there by my side.

Soon after, I was busy computing range tables for weapons systems, which was in line with the traditional ordnance development role of the facility. Several new missions were emerging as the technological world was changing. The satellite era, as they called it, brought with it many changes and career-advancing opportunities for scientists and mathematicians like us, but only our white counterparts were being recognized. That was disheartening, but we didn't let it stop us. I didn't have any mentors to help me get through situations like this and give me advice on how to handle the disappointments, as the more experienced workers and supervisors were all white, so they never really spent time with us, as this was all new to them, and most of them were not comfortable talking to us and giving us individual guidance. I realized that I had to make it on my own, so I just kept working hard. Despite not getting the "good" work assignments time and time again, I stayed motivated by thinking about a rule I had lived by since high school – never be satisfied with being number two.

I was also going through a very difficult pregnancy, so I prayed for strength, and reflected on a favorite verse - "I can do all things through Christ who strengthens me" – Philippians 4:13. Ira prayed with me, and on Sundays, we went to Chapel as we always had, but it was feeling more and more meaningful now. Toward the end of my pregnancy term, I was at home on maternity leave. One day I was feeling some pain, so I called Ira, thinking it may be time, although I wasn't feeling any kicking from the baby the way I had been for several months. Something just didn't feel right. We said a prayer, and Ira immediately rushed me to the hospital, but this day would end tragically. After making it almost to full term, I had lost the baby. It was a stillbirth. As far back as I could remember, I had never imagined this happening, and neither did Ira, but some things that we take for granted in life are not as certain as we think. I found that out so painfully when I lost my child. Ira and I tried to comfort each other that night, and we called Ma Macy to tell her the sad news, which was so hard to do, especially since we had just lost my Daddy. We asked her to inform the others. We kept blaming ourselves at first, wondering what we did wrong, but then after speaking with some of our family members and worshiping at Chapel, we were able to pull ourselves together. "God will let us know when the time is right," Ira said, even though he was hurting just as much as I was. He was there for me, though, making sure I was alright, my rock as always, and my best friend. The ladies in the club were very supportive and so were my other co-workers, and my sorority sister and good friend, Pearl.

I continued to read my scriptures and go to Chapel on Sundays. We decided that we would try again after about six months. Before long, I was pregnant again, and Ira was once again taking good care of me.

(Above) This was the first building I worked in at Dahlgren.

The Test and Proof Gun Line. This testing could be heard, and vibrations felt at certain times of the day at Dahlgren.

At our Boomtown home in Dahlgren.   Signs like this were still a reality off base.

Ma Macy at the home in North Dinwiddie after church. She will always be my role model.

My early days in Boomtown that I remember so well.

CHAPTER FIVE: BARRIERS BROKEN

Technology within the Federal Government was growing by leaps and bounds. The National Aeronautics and Space Administration (NASA) had already been established several months earlier under President Eisenhower on July 29, 1958, as a result of the space race between the USA and the Soviet Union. It was created from the National Advisory Committee for Aeronautics and other related organizations. Its purpose was to develop non-military space programs. The NRL Vanguard group, a total of approximately 200 scientists and engineers, was moved to NASA and became the core of its Space Flight activities. The group remained housed at NRL because the new facilities at the Goddard Space Flight Center at Greenbelt, Maryland, were not due to become available until September 1960.

Vanguard II launched on February 17, 1959 and was the first satellite designed to observe and record the cloud cover of the earth. It was a forerunner of the television infrared observation satellites (TIROS). Vanguard II was also the first full-scale Vanguard (20-inch sphere, 21 pounds) to be launched, and it is still in orbit to this day. The scientific experiments flown on the Vanguard satellites increased scientific knowledge of space and opened the way for more sophisticated experiments. Vanguard was the prototype for much of what became the U.S. space program.

We were becoming more comfortable with Dahlgren as the days, weeks, and months went by. Ira was working busily with the new submarine-based missiles program, and I was busy computing algorithms that were created by some of the many brilliant people who had come aboard to study an array of new projects that we had been tasked with. Dahlgren and the Naval Research Laboratory had some of the best and brightest minds in science and math, and Ira and I were honored to be amongst them. It was a time when we had been through World War II, the Korean War, and now we were in the Cold War and Space Race, so working for the Defense, whether military or research and development, was very attractive. We all felt we were doing something very important for America.

I was also moving along with my second pregnancy, hoping that this time things would be better, giving us the child we were praying for. We felt the biggest thing that could help with our grief of losing the first child would be to have a successful childbirth this second time around. We were making sure I was eating right and taking care of my overall health. I was also reading books and any articles I could find about pregnancy. The mixed emotions of losing the first child and then trying again made it a very anxious time, so we chose not to tell most of the people at Dahlgren that I was pregnant again until I was about 18 weeks. If it was possible to have gone through the whole pregnancy without telling anyone, and then announce a new baby, that is what I would have done.

I was getting bigger, and my job responsibilities had grown as well, and my role on the team had become more independent. It was easy to withdraw into my own professional world in a situation like this, so I made a special effort to continue to have good relationships with my supervisor, and with my co-workers. Communication can play a very big part in the culture of an organization. It is like its foundation. Scientists, mathematicians, and technical people can sometimes get lost in their specific tasks and forget how important it is for everyone to communicate with one another. This was more particularly so for some of the more brilliant minds that made up our organization, whose genius came from their tendency to be individualists and freethinkers. As a woman in that environment of mostly white males, it was important to stay in tune, ask questions, and be responsive when problems would arise. That was something I thought would help to get me noticed.

Ira and I hoped to get assigned to some of the work that involved travel, but it never seemed to happen. Then one day we were talking to our colleague, Herman Caster, and he mentioned that he had been on one trip with his team, but there was a problem when he got to the hotel where the others were staying; he was not allowed to stay there – It was for whites only. Again, there was still segregation and discrimination in our Nation, and to spare the embarrassment, our higher-ups decided that they would not ask the black professionals to travel. It was very competitive, so those travel assignments were opportunities where you could shine and show your worth. We did not get the opportunity to show what we could do in such settings as we were not getting sent out on those assignments. Travel was also good for professional development as well.

We continued to talk as a couple at home about situations that involved race or gender. Every now and then, we shared our concerns with some other colleagues of color, but not with our white peers, because you didn't really know who your friends were, so we rarely discussed things of that nature at work. We also realized that we had to look at it from management's standpoint because they had to get the work accomplished, and if they thought there would be a problem outside the Dahlgren gates with us traveling and staying overnight, then they would give the work to someone else where travel would not be problematic. In those days though, we were low men and women on the totem pole, so we came into these jobs knowing things like this were going to happen...especially if you were a woman.

Mr. Niemann recognized the early potential for using computers to solve massive technical problems and led the implementation of cumbersome exterior ballistics calculations on a succession of "super" computers. Under his direction, the department at Dahlgren led the field in the Fleet Ballistic Missile Program. As a result of knowing the importance of computers at Dahlgren, the people who had been there a while would talk about other people in the industry who were doing great things. I was hearing about a woman who had been a pioneer in proving that women could get the job done in non-traditional roles in technology and mathematics. Her name was Grace Brewster Murray Hopper, a computer pioneer, and naval officer. The "Queen of Code" as she was sometimes referred to, Hopper received a master's degree and a Ph.D. in mathematics from Yale after first receiving her undergraduate degree from Vassar. One of the first three modern programmers, she is best known for her trailblazing contributions to the development of computer languages. She was the daughter of a Phi Beta Kappa scholar from Yale and grew up in New York City, and she had long and influential careers in both the U.S. Navy and the private sector. She came of age in the 1920s and 1930s, a time when relatively high numbers of women were receiving doctorates. Numbers that would not be matched again until the 1980s. World War II also created opportunities for women to enter the workforce in greater numbers as well. Her success in a male-dominated field and in almost all-male organizations, including the U.S. Navy, was exceptional. During World War II, Hopper took a leave of absence from teaching at Vassar and joined the Naval Reserve in 1943.

Hopper was responsible for programming the Mark I and punching machine instructions onto tape. The close relationship between the U.S. military and the early computer industry, nurtured first by World War II and then by the Cold War, shaped her career path. She was largely given credit for the success of COBOL, the first standardized, general business computer language that started in 1959. Women like Hopper helped the cause of other women like me who were moving forward, earn respect, and break down barriers in the male-dominated fields of science and math at this time in our history. There was one thing – Hopper was White. As a Black woman, I had the double unfair treatment working against me, which was my race and my gender. With the typical role of black women at the time largely being housewives, domestics, clerical workers, and if educated, teachers in the segregated school systems, that made it even more difficult to be successful in the science and mathematics fields. It sure didn't hurt that Hopper was ahead of all of us, though, leading the way and at least breaking gender barriers in a grand way. I kept thinking that one day I would work for a woman supervisor – or be a supervisor myself.

I was determined to do my best, and I worked as hard as anyone on my team, despite advancing well into my second pregnancy. The workforce, in those days, was not very family or maternity friendly. I heard there were some managers at other agencies or workplaces that did not want to hire women who were in the typical childbearing ages, because it would disrupt the flow of the work when someone would have to take leave for a certain amount of time. That is another thing that made it more difficult for women to get employed in professional positions then, much less be promoted into supervisory jobs. There was no work at home program back then, no leave donation programs, and I had not been working long enough to have earned a lot of leave. I was going into the office building every day, which was only a short walk or shuttle ride away from where we lived in Boomtown. I was in my last trimester of the pregnancy, and I was thinking to myself… *if only I could get through these last couple of months.* I was getting extra monitoring and extra care, but at the time, medical technology was not as advanced as it is today. Ira was working on some very interesting projects with the missile program, and I was working with some very brilliant, almost genius-level people, who were developing all types of algorithms for studies. We had to do the work to compute them.

We always came home in the evenings and talked about our days and the work at the office, but ultimately the discussion always shifted to how I was feeling. Ira was very good about checking on me, showing his concern, and being empathetic of my needs without worrying me. It was his calm approach that helped me a lot through those difficult days. He made sure I made all my Ob/Gyn appointments, as we had been told that it was always a possibility this pregnancy could be just as difficult as the first one. My anxiety level was significantly high, as you can imagine, but we wanted a family, so we were willing to try this again and pray for the best possible outcome. I kept thinking that God had brought us together for a reason. We did not know what the future held, but we knew that he was preparing us for something special – possibly more special than the work we were doing at Dahlgren. The weeks continued to go by, and as I was getting closer to the due date. My work was important to me, and it was good for me because it tended to take my mind off the discomforts of childbearing. Every day it seemed I was thinking only about two things – doing outstanding work as a mathematician and preparing for the birth of our child. By this time, I had even blocked out the piercing sounds and vibrations from the guns and artillery that were tested daily, fired from the installation's proving range southward into the Potomac River. However, it was hard sometimes to ignore some of the things that I heard from unknowing colleagues. No one understands what you are going through unless they have been through it themselves. There were co-workers, family, and friends who were asking all kinds of questions, and saying, "It will be alright this time." Some folks didn't know whether to congratulate me or pray for me, but I realized they all meant well. I was looking now to my faith for strength and to Ira and my immediate family for their constant love, comfort, and support. I was confident that it was in God's hands, and I knew that he would be with me every step of the way.

I was only a couple weeks from the due date when I noticed the baby had not been kicking like before. We remembered that we were to go immediately to the hospital if there was no movement inside the womb for a long period of time. I called my doctor, and Ira drove me to the hospital. It felt the same as the first time, but I was still hoping and praying for the best. When we arrived at the hospital in Petersburg, there were several people there who rushed me to the maternity ward. I was in a lot of pain at this point, and they sent Ira to a waiting room, so I did not have his hand to hold. I could feel my heart racing, but no movement of the baby as the nurses and doctor were preparing me for what was obviously a C-section delivery. I recall the look on their faces. It was a look of urgency while trying to comfort and calm me at the same time. I don't remember much after that except going in and out as I was waking up from the effects of the anesthetics. I was in recovery and feeling very sore, when I was told by my doctor that I lost the baby. For the second time, in less than two years, the baby had not survived. Ira was there holding my hand as the doctor remained close by with his clipboard, and that's when I sensed there was more. He said that he had to perform a hysterectomy at the same time. Ira noticed my saddened look of disbelief, moved in closer, and interjected that I was in danger of bleeding to death, so the doctor had no choice but to remove my uterus. The doctor continued to explain more to me about what had happened, but I didn't hear a word. I just looked into Ira's eyes and he looked at mine. I would not be able to conceive a child now, and that was all that was on my mind.

I was thinking maybe this was just some bad dream that will go away, but the more he squeezed my hand and held me closer to him, the further I realized it was real. I remember my daddy holding me that way when I was a little girl, as he whispered in my ear to be strong after a bee sting or a bad cold. He wasn't there now, but Ira was just as comforting, and I felt safe in his arms. I was in that hospital for several more days and then spent almost six more weeks at home recovering. I did a lot of thinking during that time. After all, there wasn't much more I could do while recuperating. I prayed and asked why me. I would be a good mother, I thought, even better than Ma Macy, at least from a financial point, because I would have more to offer a child due to my salary and professional potential. I know Ira was still very disappointed, but he tried not to show it. He was there for me again, and so was Ma Macy, my sister Annie, and so many others who helped get me back on my feet. I began to reflect on my Daddy's qualities, and how he had taught me, by example, to have a certain mental toughness through grief and adversity. I also thought about how Ma Macy and the rest of the family needed me. I began to pray more often as well, when I was alone, and with Ira. The more I prayed, I realized that God had a plan for me, and my dream was still there. Besides, I had to get back to my office and prove some things, to the Navy and to myself.

We were still working with those large computers that had to be fed by punch cards. All the punch cards had to be checked. These early computers, such as the IBM 7090, were operated at the machine language level, and had their own programming language. Despite all that I had endured over the last couple of years, I knew that I still had so much to be thankful for, and I tried to concentrate on my work at Dahlgren. I must have been placed there for a reason, I thought to myself. After all, I was black and a female. Was I just there as an experiment? Was I placed here to just be a mathematician, and not raise a family like my mother had done so well? Those thoughts crossed my mind occasionally, but I tried my best to tune them out and concentrate on what needed to be done. When you are one of the first to get an opportunity like I was given, you are a trailblazer for all who will follow you. You must prove that you not only could carry out your responsibilities satisfactorily but go beyond what is expected and perform at a high level. Barriers must be broken. I committed myself to that, as a lot of people back home were counting on me. Another year had come around before we knew it. We had moved into a new decade; the space race was growing rapidly, and the civil rights movement was making huge strides. John F. Kennedy was our new President, and we were all so excited. However, there was some other news that came at the end of the year, even more exciting for us. We had bought a new Chevy, and traded in the old one, in anticipation of increasing our family size by one. Yes, after months of discussing and praying about it, we decided that we would adopt a child, maybe two eventually. It was the right thing to do. To share all the blessings that had been bestowed on us. There is a line of wisdom that reads, "To whom much is given, much will be required" (Luke 12:48). When we are blessed with talents, wealth, knowledge, time, and the like, it is expected that we benefit others. That was us – young, educated, black profession-als, with good incomes. When Ralph Niemann hired us into positions that folks who looked like us had never held before at Dahlgren, it made our lives different from most black residents in Virginia – and quite frankly most whites as well. We weren't exactly the "Talented Tenth" as Dubois had pinned it almost 60 years earlier, but we were better off than most people of color at that time. We knew it would be a long process, and there would be much to learn, but it would be worth it. We were ready to be parents to some deserving children who needed our love and provisions; and who most certainly deserved a family, as much as we desired one. It took me a while to understand the disappointment of los-ing my birth children, but now I was starting to feel God working through me, and it was time to look for a reputable agency that would help us every step of the way.

President Kennedy was inaugurated January 20, 1961, and there were big expectations in America. Despite all our ills as a country, I believed we were moving forward as a nation, and something Kennedy said at his inauguration has stayed with me to this day. "Ask not what your country can do for you—ask what you can do for your country." It was so profound at that moment, and I believe it was a wake-up call to Americans. No matter your race, religion, gender, or walk of life, you have an obligation and opportunity to do something great for you and for the world, and that will always resonate with me.

With so much hope for the future, Ira and I both were happy with the probability of contributing to society and doing what we could for the country. I kept thinking about how fortunate I was to have prepared myself to be in a position to do just that at Dahlgren. We were excited. We were also excited about finding a child that we could bring into our family after being told about an adoption agency in Alexandria, Virginia. Ma Macy was happy for us as well. She told us that we could make a difference in a child's life, especially because of the type of people we were. She said we could provide a good life for a child.

We were still spending time on the weekends with Ma Macy and my brothers. My brother Joseph had children who were becoming close to us. We had even kept the two oldest over the weekend with us a few times and for a week or so during the prior summer months. It gave us a chance to see what living with and caring for children might be like for us. The adoption agency also advised us that experience with children is useful to all new parents. We could learn what to expect of ourselves and of a child. They told us no parent automatically knows the details of taking care of a child, what to expect, or how to handle emergencies that tend to occur in daily living. The counseling they provided to prospective parents was priceless. They also recommended that we find a family member or friend, just as a biological mother would do after giving birth, from whom we could seek help or support. We both agreed that Ma Macy would be that person for us without a doubt. Making the decision to adopt was more than a notion, but we were ready to start our family.

Spring had arrived, with all its colorful charm and natural splendor, and we were learning more about being parents and were preparing for our new addition to the family as summer approached. Ira was getting some good experience while helping to coach the community little league baseball team. He was so good with those boys and seemed to really enjoy it. It was then that I knew he was going to be a great father, although he had never had much fathering himself. We even started teaching Sunday school at the Dahlgren Chapel and were able to interact with our co-workers' children, especially the Caster and Jones children, who we had become very familiar with. Soon after we celebrated our 5th wedding anniversary, we were making progress with the adoption agency and decided that a girl would be our first choice. Ira said a girl to carry on my legacy and that of Ma Macy would be perfect. President Kennedy had proposed the moon program and pledged to land a man on the moon by the end of the decade. There was so much promise, and I felt like I was on cloud nine when the adoption agency told us they had found the perfect little girl for us. We were told that they had the perfect baby girl, only a few months old, that they wanted us to meet. We drove to Alexandria, Virginia, to visit her that week, in anticipation of working out the administrative and legal details and becoming her parents.

It was a beautiful sunny morning when we arrived in Alexandria, for our visit to the adoption agency. I remember thinking, "This must be the day." I was a little nervous, but no more than any other mother to be. We were directed right away to the nursery area to see the baby that they thought would be a match. We looked at her and knew right away that this was our little miracle. She was beautiful, and within minutes I knew she was the one. Ira was almost speechless, and it's not easy at all to see him lost for words. We looked at each other, and without saying much at all, we knew that our prayers had been answered. As Ira wrapped his arms around me, the representative asked if we wanted to start the process, and we nodded with approval. We took turns holding her, and then it was on to the office to find out more about how to proceed. It was about four weeks before little Carolyn, as we named her, was in our home and our own baby girl. We were so filled with joy to be a family. We took her to meet Ma Macy and Ira's mom, Blanche. They both felt so bad for me after the hysterectomy at such a young age. They were happy for me now, as they called me "Mom" while hugging and welcoming their new grandchild. The hugs and kisses that our new baby girl was receiving were abundant from family, friends, and especially from Ira and me. Carolyn brought so much joy to our hearts with each new day. Her warm smile was all I had dreamed about, and I felt so blessed to be her Mom.

We could not personally tell everyone of our good news, but we sent announcements to friends, coworkers, and family, as advised by the adoption agency. Ira's job responsibilities were growing, and so were mine, so it was important that we talked to our supervisors directly to inform them of our addition at home. We already had a housekeeper who came in on a monthly basis, and although we were both able to walk home for lunch, another lady was also needed at the house every workday to care for Carolyn. It was fun watching Carolyn through most of her developmental stages. She crawled, she walked, and of course she said "da-da" first.

I was enjoying Carolyn as she grew older. Picking out her clothes and fixing her hair were my favorites. I'm sure I got that from observing my Ma Macy. Carolyn was developing her own personality and Ira and I were starting to communicate to her with words and expressions. The bond between us as a family was a wonderful thing to watch develop. It was interesting times at the West household, as we loved our little girl and she loved us back. My work at Dahlgren was getting more interesting as well. Some of the new projects did not seem to be as related to defense or satellite navigation as they had in the past. The focus of my work was more to understand the fundamental nature of orbits and gravity. It was exciting to be involved in more than programming and coding. I was beginning to feel more respected for my abilities. Nevertheless, it was a bit disconcerting to see my male counterparts moving into leadership roles and assigned to more challenging projects than the women, especially for me as a black woman. Men seemed to be rewarded more for their passion and commitment to the job, but that was not the case for women. The men who were tough were considered competent. If a woman like me was viewed as assertive or passionate, then she was considered angry or not management material. I always kept that in the back of my mind as I went about performing my duties at the office. I did not want to be perceived as hostile, having a bad day, and not taken seriously. So even when things weren't going so well at home with a sick child, or the baby-sitter not showing up, I could not show it, which made my job more difficult than theirs.

I was also enjoying the progress that President Kennedy was making with his so-called "new generation of Americans." He showed great leadership during the Cuban Missile Crisis in 1962, as he was able to get the Soviet Union to remove the missiles from Cuba. At home, his stand on the civil rights movement was courageous. He believed it to be the moral, constitutional, and legal thing to do. He addressed the nation on the struggle to affirm civil rights for all Americans during the summer of 1963. He vowed to submit legislation to Congress to end segregation in education and guarantee the right to vote for all. Ira and I were happy to hear of this commitment led by Kennedy, and the prospect of better things to come for our little girl's future. However, there were others who were not happy with the direction the country was going under Kennedy. The basic ideals that were important to him, were too liberal in the eyes of those who preferred the status quo be maintained.

We were all excited about Dr. Martin Luther King Jr. and his rise to prominence in the civil rights movement. He delivered the "I Have a Dream" speech during the March on Washington for jobs and freedom in late August of that same year. Dr. King called for civil and economic rights and an end to racism in America, and many celebrities were by his side in support and some like Bob Dylan, Joan Baez, and one of my favorites, Mahalia Jackson, performed. I heard later that current Congressman John Lewis spoke that day as well. Neither Ira and I, nor the other black mathematicians at Dahlgren joined the 250,000 others who were

117

there on that hot summer day in Washington, DC. Since there were not many people of color in secret classified positions, we felt it would be better not to get involved in civil rights events like this event, but our hearts and desires for change were there more than ever. It was very important in our opinion that we continue to prove our worth in performing the work we were doing for the Federal Government so that other people of color would be considered when jobs became available. My favorite words from that speech by King were, "I have a dream that my four little children will one day live in a nation where they will not be judged by the color of their skin but by the content of their character." That part of the speech was so important to me because I always believed that a person's character and values tell almost everything about them, and I hope all people choose to pass that on to their children as I have to my own.

On November 22, 1963, President Kennedy was assassinated in Dallas, Texas. He was riding in a presidential motorcade with his wife Jacqueline and Texas Governor, John Connally, when he was fatally shot by a gunman from a nearby building. He was pronounced dead at a nearby hospital 30 minutes later. Connally was also shot, but he recovered. Lee Harvey Oswald was arrested and was charged that same day. Vice President Lyndon B. Johnson automatically assumed the Presidency and was sworn in on Air Force One. America had never witnessed anything like this since the television era had begun. It was a sad day in America, and we were all in our homes sitting around televisions that evening, holding back tears, and trying to come to grips with this senseless act of violence. All the hope and promise that Kennedy stood for was gone in an instant. America still wonders whether Oswald acted alone or not in the assassination, but it was only the first of many tragic events of the 60s.

It was a very solemn time, but I had to continue being a good mother and wife, and there was so much ahead with a new astronomical study that I was working on. I was on a team that was tasked with looking at the orbit of the planet Pluto, in relation to Neptune. This required 5 billion calculations, or 100 hours of processing time. With the computing power of today, it might not be such an enormous task, but at that time, Project 29V, as it was known, was only possible through the efforts of our team of amazing mathematicians and myself. We received a group achievement award for the work we did on that project, and in the same year a new building opened for the computational analysis division. It was Building 1200, and we were all so proud of that building at the time – although in recent years, it was discovered that the builders used asbestos in the building, so it had to be raised.

Soon after the new building was dedicated, Carolyn turned three years old, and President Johnson signed the Civil Rights Act of 1964. It was based on the initial legislation that John F. Kennedy had suggested, outlawing discrimination in public facilities, and in hotels and restaurants, and prohibiting employment discrimination based on race, ethnicity, religion, or gender. Later that year, Johnson was reelected by a landslide in the November 1964 election. On Aug 6, 1965, Johnson signed the Voting Rights Act of 1965. The act abolishes literacy tests and other tests used by local and state governments to inhibit African American voting. Things like civil rights and the space program were certainly positives in our nation, but not everything was good. The Vietnam War was escalating. There was an increased U.S. military presence, and

Americans were losing their lives daily. On the civil rights side, Muslim minister and human rights activist Malcolm X had been assassinated while delivering a speech in Harlem – another senseless act of violence.

Carolyn was four years old now, and we were enjoying seeing her grow and learn so fast. Ira said she was beginning to take on my characteristics, which made me smile. She just picked up everything so quickly, and we realized in less than a year, she would be in kindergarten at the Dahlgren School on base. Our work was important, but she was our priority and the joy of our lives. The summer after her birthday, we picked up Jackie and Francine, Joseph's oldest girls, and they stayed with us for a couple of weeks. We always thought it was good to give them a chance to see life outside of Sutherland, you know, good exposure. They seemed to enjoy it too, except Jackie said we were big on discipline, so they had to behave like young ladies when they were visiting Dahlgren. She loved being able to dress up more though, something she only did on Sundays at home. They never really knew what Ira and I did when we went into that office building because we could not discuss our work with anyone outside of the base, but they knew it was something differ-ent. It was wonderful to see them bonding with Carolyn, so we could not help but think how nice it would be if she had a sibling. We decided we would wait to make that decision during the Christmas holidays, as we would have more time to discuss it together during our vacation.

After spending our Christmas vacation with Ma Macy and the family, we stopped in Petersburg to visit the Hunters on our way back to Dahlgren, as we usually did during the holidays. While listening to some of Dr. (John) Hunter's jokes, we sampled some of his holiday season specialty – Pig's feet, or as he called them "trotters." He slow cooked those trotters to perfection, adding in a little of his own tasty barbeque sauce. Served with his wife's collard greens and potato salad, he reminded us that you can't eat too many pig's feet because they were low in fat and high in protein. That's all Ira needed to hear, and he looked forward to that dish every year. Now, remember this was a Physics Professor with these cooking skills. I guess you just don't know about a man until you sit down in his kitchen and enjoy some of his soul food. That day we shared with them our interest in adopting another child. They thought it was a great idea, and that it would be a good idea for Carolyn to have a sibling. They also asked if we had thought about the extra time and attention it would take to care for two children; being with them when they are sick; getting them involved in activities and so on, with both of us being professionals with very demanding careers. They were similarly situated, with both being high profile college professors, so that's probably why they only had one child. On the one hand, they were saying go for it, and on the other hand, they were saying if you do it, make sure you can handle it. It was great advice, as many women in the past were not pursuing professional careers, so it was not as difficult for them to have more children and care for them. It seems there were more women at this time in our history who desired both, and I happened to be one of them.

In 1966, we decided to adopt again, this time a boy, and we named him David Ira West. We went back to the same adoption agency since we were so familiar with them. It was a lot easier this time and before we knew it, David, who was about 5 months old, was part of our family. Everyone was excited to see us with the two children, Ira holding David, and Carolyn holding my hand. That became a typical sight to see around Boomtown. Carolyn started kindergarten a few months after David became a part of our family. She was at the Dahlgren Base School. We had a lady who took care of David during the day, and she would be there in the evening when we came home. We also came home for lunch on workdays, since the building was a short walk from our house. There was always time every day for David and Carolyn despite our busy work schedules. They were both active, and Carolyn was also developing into a very good student in school. She was also involved in activities like swimming and piano.

Soon Ira and I would sit down with Carolyn to discuss the "birds and the bees," if you will. We wanted her to understand how David became her brother and our family member, without her hearing things from schoolmates and other family members. We wanted her to know that she was adopted as well. There was a book that was given to us by the adoption agency when we were in the process of bringing Carolyn into our family. It was called, The Adopted Family, and had two volumes, one for parents, and the other The Family That Grew, that you could read with the children. It served as a guide for adoptive parents and was a great resource for parents to read to their children and explain the situation that made them a family. I felt more relaxed and at ease discussing it with the children while I had that book in my hand. Carolyn enjoyed the stories in the book such as lines like this,"…how a man and a lady start every little baby, but sometimes something happens that they cannot take care of the baby they started, so they find a father and mother to love and take care of the baby." Carolyn and I discussed that book several times, and when I would sit down and read it to David, several years later, she was right there beside me, helping to explain it to her little brother.

About a year and a half later, we received a phone call from the adoption agency. The representative was following up on how things were going with Carolyn and David, but that was not all. She also informed us that there was a three-month-old boy whose young single mother and her family had no means to care for him. The child was available for adoption, and she said there was no better family that could take this child into their home than us. She was convinced that this child would be a better fit with Carolyn and David, and that there were not many black couples in their system with our character, experience, and salaries who could care for another child. She wanted us to consider adding one more child who could be a younger brother to Carolyn and David. We told her we would get back to her. We both felt honored that the agency thought so highly of us. We also knew there would not be many other black couples who could take another child into their family as we were capable of doing. It was so hard to say no – I guess I was like Ma Macy in that way, always giving and caring for others. Ira, who liked that about me, was very similar himself, especially when it came to children, so within a couple of weeks, we decided to take yet another infant into our family and give our children another sibling. It was a blessing to have this opportunity to give back, especially considering how much better situated we were than most black couples at that time. We named him Michael Scott West (Scott was Ma Macy's maiden name) and gave him the same love and attention that we had given to Carolyn and David. We were now a family of five, with plenty of love to share, and lots of prayers going up every day.

I was very transparent with my supervisor about my parenting responsibilities, but this was all a learning process for him because his wife did not work. This idea of women being mothers and career women was new to many of the men who were managers in the workforce, even in the 60s. I also wanted him to know by my work production that I was very committed to my career and wanted to be valued not only as an employee but as a future leader in the organization. He also was aware that Ira was going to be helping with the kids as well, taking them to doctor's appointments and sharing other responsibilities that mothers traditionally handled. Ira stepped up big time, and I think that was an important factor in me being able to handle the challenges of motherhood, and a profession previously dominated by men. I wanted to prove that I could be the best mathematician and the best mother, at the same time. It was time for some barriers to be broken, and why not me to be the one to break them?

1968 was another year of tragic events in our country's history. On April 4, 1968, Martin Luther King was assassinated in Memphis, Tennessee. Black Americans responded to his death in different ways, as most were devastated and angered. Violence, riots, and looting broke out in over one hundred American cities. Troops were sent in to stop the violence, but there were several people killed and a few thousand injured. We were all glued to our television sets, as we were before when we lost President Kennedy. It was frustrating to see people so angry that they were damaging property in their own neighborhoods. Some business communities in the large urban cities looked as if a bomb had been dropped on them. Many white Americans were saddened, but there were others who were untouched, some even calling Dr. King a "troublemaker." We were wondering how our white colleagues at Dahlgren and in our Boom Town community would respond, and we quickly found most of them to be very saddened and appalled. They seemed to be a little nervous about the violence that was occurring around the country and did not seem to want to talk about it, but they seemed to feel safe within the confines of the Naval Base. I felt safe, too, behind those security gates, but I was a little worried about Ma Macy and my family members in Dinwiddie County, but after talking to them by telephone, they reassured us that there were no violent incidents at home. I was also concerned about the safety of former co-worker Orbie Jones and his family. He had accepted a position with NASA a few years prior and moved his family to Washington, DC, which was experiencing widespread rioting and violence. Former co-worker Clara had relocated to California with her husband, and we were hoping they were safe as well.

After King's death, the Black Power movement took on a new energy. Black Americans were even more distrustful of white institutions and the American political system. When I watched the television coverage of the funeral with Dr. King's young children there, clinging to their mother, I could not help but look at my children, hold them close to me and protect them. What would I say to them, and would they understand? I concluded that the answer to that question was "no" because I did not understand these turbulent times myself. We had never experienced anything like this as people of color in America, but just looking at the outpouring of love and support coming from the most influential black celebrities and leaders in America of that time, I realized history was being made, but we weren't done yet.

LBJ decided not to seek election for another term as president, and John F. Kennedy's brother Robert was the favorite to win the Democratic nomination for president. He had the charisma of his older brother and seemed even more liberal on issues regarding civil rights and discrimination towards minorities and women. While campaigning in California and winning that state's primary, tragedy would strike again, as Robert F. Kennedy was assassinated on June 6, 1968. Dr. King had been assassinated in the Spring, igniting riots and anger across the country, and now another rising star, who had pledged to end many of the discriminatory practices that were dividing our country was violently gunned down. He had so much promise, but he never got another opportunity. The same decade that we started our family with three wonderful little children was marred with so much violence and the loss of some great men. At what point would it all end – and what was to come in the next decade?

We were both enjoying the children and watching them grow and develop into their own little selves. The work at Dahlgren was getting more interesting and gratifying as well. Ira continued work on the missiles program, and I continued to work on computer software that processed geoid heights, or precise surface elevations. It was 1969 and Richard Nixon was our new president. The war in Vietnam had peaked, and we were trying to put a man on the moon in the space program. Ira and I had started to look for houses about this time as our family size had obviously increased. We searched in the King George, Virginia area, which was only a few miles away from the Dahlgren base but without much luck. Outside of those Dahlgren gates, we were still in the south. Virginia had integrated or was in the process of doing so by this time, but homes that had been built prior to integration had "restricted covenants" attached to their deeds. Additionally, mortgage companies and banks were continuing to discriminate against blacks who were trying to move into established neighborhoods that remained white.

Here again was another hurdle to overcome in our pursuit to simply be good parents, citizens, and professionals. Many of our young black men were serving in the Vietnam War for our country, and this is what they had to look forward to when or if they made it back home. Ira had to be thinking about that every time we heard the word "no" in our house buying search. He had served in the Army during the Korean War and was now working on some highly classified technical projects for the Navy and our country, yet he was being turned down by mortgage companies because of the color of his skin. It appeared the more things changed, the more they remained the same. Don't get me wrong, we were angry, but somehow, we had something inside us that kind of kept us in the fight. We refused to take the low road or give up. There were too many people counting on us.

How would we discuss these situations with our children? That was a question that often crossed our minds. Life for them was a lot easier behind these gates, but how would they be able to handle the racially intimidating areas on the outside. Carolyn was doing very well at the Dahlgren School, but by this time, she was in second grade, and there were no other black classmates. It never seemed to bother her though, and we never made a big deal about it. Though we kind of knew she was breaking barriers herself, and doing it quite well, I'm proud to say, there would be a time where things would be more difficult for her, and that's what I was hoping to prepare her for, by being a good example myself.

127

The boys were younger, so I was thinking by the time they got older, there would be integration everywhere and very little discrimination.

The big news of the day was about Neil Armstrong setting foot on the Moon, fulfilling JFK's pledge to land a man on the moon by the end of the decade. Yes, the USA had beat the Soviet Union by landing the first human on the Moon. It was amazing to watch this unbelievable scene on television, and each time I saw the footage, it became more astonishing. I had no idea back then that Katherine Johnson and those other black ladies from Margot Lee Shetterly's book, Hidden Figures, were behind the scenes doing a lot of the math involved in making that mission a success. Here I was thinking I was one of the few black women working in the mathematics field for the federal government, but there were more, several more evidently. I had often wondered how exciting it would be to work at NASA, especially since one of our black mathematicians left Dahlgren and moved to the much talked about Goddard Space Flight Center in Maryland. If I had known these ladies from the book were over at the NASA Langley Research Center, I may have considered making the move there. I loved my life at Dahlgren, but I wanted more responsibility and an opportunity to manage and things just seemed to be moving slow for me there because I was a black female – Two strikes against me, but I had to be a good "two-strike hitter" as Ira would sometimes say. If I kept my eyes open and remained patient, something good was bound to happen.

Speaking of patience, we were wondering what to do if we could not move into a neighborhood outside of the base. Then we found some land that was available on a country road in King George. What made this piece of land different was what made it worth the wait. The land was in a wooded area and owned by a black family. We knew this was only God leading us to this ten-acre property that had been vacant for years, it seemed. It was situated in a tucked away, more remote area of King George, but it was perfect for us. I'm not sure how and when those black folks had acquired that land, but it was all ours now. We had been saving for this opportunity, so we paid cash to purchase it. It was a blessing how it all happened, and now we had to make plans to build a house that would be our home for a long time.

Herman Caster and his family moved to a new home about this time, close to the base and located on Route 206. My Soror Pearl and her husband, who were working at Dahlgren, moved into the Bayberry Estates development off Route 301. The builder of that development was not discriminating because they were new homes, and they had to abide by the fair housing laws. They offered financing as well. We did not want a house in the new development because we wanted to be in a more spacious area and build our home. After we purchased the land, we felt relieved and had a clearer picture about our next step, which was to build a house with more space. In the next few months, we made decisions on when to build on the property and who to have as the builder. After receiving some good news, we decided not to build right away. We had already moved into a larger house on base in a residential section called Tarrytown, a community of upgraded single-family homes, not far from Boomtown. It was for higher grade level civilian workers and active military officers. It felt strange not living in Boomtown, which had been our home since we were married, but we were still on base and ran into many of our previous neighbors at the office and while visiting the school, the chapel, and shopping at the stores on base. It was also hard to believe we had been married for more than twelve years, too. I guess time flies when you marry the right person. Hopefully, Ira was thinking the same about me.

We were moving right along as a family, and I was feeling blessed to have Ira by my side. It seemed the children were adjusting to the bigger house better than us. Carolyn was coming into her own, playing the piano beautifully, swimming competitively on the base, and on the honor roll in school. She also competed for my attention when Joseph's girls would come to visit, and when we visited Ma Macy on weekends. I spent a lot of time helping Jackie, Francine, and Cheryl with their homework, and teaching them how to do different chores around Ma Macy's house, so they had become attached to me, as much as they were to Ma Macy, who they spent a lot of time with every day. Carolyn was younger than them and got a little jealous sometimes when she felt they were getting more attention. I noticed it and so did Ira, so we made sure we let Carolyn know how important she was to us, especially when Joe's girls were around. David was in kindergarten and learning to swim and play sports. Carolyn was playing the big sister role with him, and that was working out well. Michael was already three years old and getting tall for his age. They were all different in many ways, but they were all Wests now, and we thanked God for that.

Along with the satisfaction that comes with being the mother of three children, I was also enjoying my job assignments and working hard to be the best on my team. I wanted to rise to a supervisory role. I knew that as a woman, and specifically a woman of color, I would have to be twice as diligent as the others to achieve that goal. The Department of Defense (DoD) had been tasked with making sure there was an accurate and stable satellite navigation system available. We took previous ideas from our own Navy scientists that called for the use of satellites to support the proposed system. For several years, I had been working extensively on projects that required taking information from the satellites to compute the shape of the earth. I was not sure why initially, but I had an idea I was working on some big things, just like Project 29V, that our team, as I previously mentioned, was recognized for accomplishing in 1964. One of my duties was to calculate the geoid, the hypothetical shape of the earth, coinciding with mean sea level and its imagined extension under, or over land areas. Thus, it was more complicated if you were getting satellite data from over water, and that is where most of my work was done. Since the earth is not perfectly round, we had to figure out the precise shape, depending on what point of the earth was being measured.

The satellites would send data from over certain areas of water, and our team would determine the precise shape of the earth of that specific area, calculating in the tides and other forces as well. This was not just to develop the all-important geoid, but also to determine precise orbits and a refined reference surface or ellipsoid, a regular geometric shape approximating the oblate shape of the earth, which can be mathematically related to the orbit references. Without these three key elements, using satellites to determine a position on Earth would not be possible. The better these elements are defined and continually refined, the better the resulting positions. My work contributed to the refinement of all three.

A geoid can be an esoteric concept to anyone outside scientific or geodetic communities. It is a model of the irregular Earth where gravity would be equal – A kind of theoretical "sea level" of gravity.

Orthometric height can be determined by knowing the geoid value for any given position, (for example, latitude or longitude, which satellites could provide) and the satellite-derived height above a reference "ellipsoid." Orthometric height is what the lay person would refer to as "elevation or elevation above sea level." Prior to satellite-based methods, determining elevations was by laborious surveying – "differential leveling" over long distances – or using barometers that could be inaccurate to hundreds of feet. There was this one moment while working on this project, when we discovered, as a team, that there was an error somewhere in the system. Nobody could figure it out, not even the big directors and scientists. After a while, I figured out where the error was located. Little me had figured out the problem before anyone else, including some folks who I considered on the "genius" level. Everyone thanked me, and I even got some applause from a few of them. It was not exactly my 15 minutes of fame as they say, because back then, we had to get it right and keep moving towards our goal. There was never time to waste, but in my mind, it was an "aha" moment that led to the solution of a problem that no one else had solved. Maybe I should have declared "eureka," but I just kept on working like it was something I did every day. I always wondered if the word had gotten back to the guys who were the designers and inventors of the GPS (Roger L. Eason, Ivan Getting, or Bradford Parkinson), but it didn't matter because colleagues who worked closely with me thought I was a hero that day, and that was like a dream come true. The work was always hard, and the whole time I was thinking, I had to be accurate, had to get it done, and get it right, but never thinking, "Oh gee, we're going to create this GPS."

We were still in an era filled with enormous societal upheaval and change. Some progress had been made, but women and minorities still faced inequality. Some good news came in 1972 regarding women's rights. After years of campaigning by feminists, Congress approved the Equal Rights Amendment (ERA) to the constitution, which read "equality of rights under the law shall not be denied or abridged by the United States or by any state on account of sex." However, the ERA was a major concern to many conservative activists who feared that it would undermine traditional gender roles. These activists mobilized against the amendment and managed to defeat it as it needed approval by legislatures in three-fourths (38) of the 50 states. Disappointments like these encouraged many women's rights activists to turn away from politics and made it difficult for women to advance in the workplace. I was in a good place though, doing some extraordinary work that very few women had been able to do. I felt blessed for the opportunity to prove my mathematical abilities in such groundbreaking scientific work for our country. I suspect I was chosen because of my drive and passion to be the best at my job. They could see the way I approached my work so responsibly, and how I worked tirelessly, every day and sometimes nights, to make sure my assignments were done right and on time. It was hard skilled work, and often thankless. It takes a special kind of dedication to do it – and get it right. Despite all that, there was no one knocking down my door, offering me a supervisory position. I was smart, competent, and committed, but I was also a black woman in an industry dominated by men, mainly white men, and that's just the way it was.

My husband and I decided to go back to school to get our master's degrees in Public Administration during this time. The University of Oklahoma had an extension program with classes offered right there on the Dahlgren base, so we both felt we could earn another degree, keep pace with our work, and still spend quality time with our children. We had a sitter for the kids and a housekeeper. That helped, and it allowed us to take some classes together. It was not going to be easy, but it was an opportunity to acquire the knowledge and management skills necessary to move up in the organization. Sometimes I think back and wonder how we did it. It must have been that drive to succeed that we had, and our way of working together as a team. Couples can accomplish so much when they work together and support each other. We were so busy raising the children, who were developing so fast, and working in the fast-paced research and analysis world of Dahlgren. I guess you could call us a power couple by this chapter in my journey. Sort of like the Hunters at Virginia State, except they really did have power. Ira graduated with his master's degree one year before me. Now I had another degree in addition to the two I had already earned before coming to Dahlgren. That was my second graduate degree, but I still had that desire to try for a doctorate degree. It was something I had thought about since meeting Dr. Louise Hunter at Virginia State.

Around this time, the GPS project was reaching new heights, so to speak, and I was starting to see the directors getting excited about what we had accomplished. They always referred to it as a team effort, and let us know we were appreciated, which meant a lot to me. Now with GPS and those models of the Earth that I helped develop, both horizontal positions and elevations can be determined within centimeters anyplace on the Earth. My teammates and I used complex algorithms to study the various forces that distort the shape of the Earth (for example, gravity, tides), and how those forces alter the path of satellite orbits. This data was extremely difficult to determine over oceans, which was of considerable interest to the Navy. It was classified work, but later we released papers that revealed the complexity of such computational concepts. I felt good about my work, although I wasn't one to toot my own horn, as Ma Macy would say. Some significant barriers had been broken, but I knew there was more to get done. However, I couldn't help but imagine that little black girl from Butterwood Road School was on a team that created something special, the GPS. Ma Macy didn't know much about what I was doing. She just knew it was math and that math was hard, so she was proud as always. Though Daddy was no longer with us, I had a feeling he would have approved.

The children were growing older, and were not babies anymore, by any means. Carolyn was very passionate about her swimming, and was a fine pianist, along with her outstanding academic achievements. She was so mature and a year away from high school. My friend Pearl said she was so much like me, just as I was like Ma Macy, but how could that be? She did not have my DNA, but she was my daughter for sure, watching me and wanting to be like her Mama. David was at that awkward age for boys, where many of the other kids in his class were outgrowing him, so he had a few problems with bullies – who were also white. Unfortunately, we still had not overcome, at least not in those white boys' minds. There were incidents at the school and in Boy Scouts. He told us about it, and that's when we had the dreaded race relations talk, which you just knew as a black parent you would have to do at some point. He seemed to get it, and he seemed to understand that he could not hold it against all white people. He had some very nice white friends, whose parents we respected, so we told him it was okay to continue being buddies with them. Ira was an assistant to the scout master and dealt with those other boys directly at a Boy Scout meeting. David never had another problem with them, at least not to his face. Our youngest child, Michael, was in school and having some difficulties. We worked with him and got him a tutor, but not much seemed to work. Finally, we were told that he was born with some learning disabilities. Once we knew that, we were able to help him more. He was also growing so much taller than Carolyn and David. Consequently, he was very athletic, and since he was the tallest kid in class, we knew he wasn't going to be bullied. We continued to go to Chapel every Sunday, teaching Sunday School and fellowshipping with the other members there. It became a big part of our children's lives, as it was for many of their classmates. Carolyn was beginning to play piano for some church events as well. I would have loved to learn to play the piano, but with our busy lives, I didn't need any other challenges at the time.

We were excited about getting started with building the new house. The problem was we had to find someone to approve a loan to build it. It was still difficult for black folks to get approved for mortgage loans in certain areas in the south. One of the white guys at the office, who was friendly with Ira, asked him if he began building the house yet. Ira told him how hard it was to get a loan to build because we were black. This fellow told Ira that he had a friend in Fredericksburg who managed a loan company. He said his friend was approving large loans to other black couples for home building and thought we should go meet with him about our dilemma. Well, we didn't waste any time driving over to Fredericksburg to meet him. Before long, we were approved for a loan, and we were planning the construction of our home on that property in King George. The first task was to clear the land and trees in the area where the house was being built, so we hired a contractor to do the job. Then Ira got my brother Nolan, Jr. to come up and help carry some of the wood and scraps away in his truck. He came up several weekends, and before I knew it, the land was clear and ready for the builder. We did a lot of the planning for this custom home, and it tickled me every time I saw Ira with that blueprint in his hand. You would think he was the building foreman himself. It seemed like every other weekend there was a contractor working on that house. I tried not to get too involved at the site, and just concentrate on the business side of things. I wasn't crazy about all that noisy drilling and hammering every weekend, but I do remember being there a few Saturdays and seeing Ira holding hands with our youngest son Michael while inspecting the framing, plumbing, and so forth. I thought to myself, "Now that is a great father-son moment." My oldest brother Joseph came up a few times to help but not as much as Nolan. Joseph had his hands full at home with a wife and six children.

At work, I was now using Doppler satellite data and was named project leader for the work done at Dahlgren with data from the Geodynamics Experimental Ocean Satellite 3, GEOS-3. The GEOS-3 provided not only Doppler data, but also early radar altimetry data, greatly improving observed surface heights for oceans. We worked with research teams from other facilities such as the Naval Research Laboratory in Washington, D.C., and all over the country. I traveled to the Wallops Island Station on Virginia's Eastern Shore to observe tests and Doppler satellite launchings a few times, but in some other places there were still barriers to business travel for me. Many hotels in the south still prohibited blacks from staying at their properties.. After all I had done for my country, there was still discrimination that I was being subjected to.

In 1976, Jimmy Carter defeated the incumbent Gerald Ford in the presidential election; Apple computer and Microsoft became incorporated, and we moved into our new house in King George. Stepping through that door of the house we hoped to call home for the rest of our lives was a momentous occasion. All our family, friends, and co-workers wanted to visit this home we had been planning and working on for several years. When Ma Macy saw the house for the first time, there were tears of joy in her eyes. She was probably thinking there is my little Gladys Mae doing things that I never thought were possible, and she was probably thinking that her Nolan, Sr. was smiling down from heaven in approval. The house was not full of furnishings and would need a few upgrades over the years, but we were happy. It was another goal we accomplished together as a team, as a family. More big things were happening at the office, too, as I was given more responsibility. We had achieved so much success with the geoid project which contributed to the success of GPS. Now even more professional achievements were ahead for Ma Macy's oldest girl.

MEAN EARTH ELLIPSOID DETERMINED FROM
SEASAT-1 ALTIMETRIC OBSERVATIONS

Gladys B. West

Naval Surface Weapons Center
Dahlgren Laboratory
Dahlgren, Virginia 22448

Prepared for presentation at the Spring American Geophysical Union
Toronto, Canada, 22-27 May 1980.

The front cover of the SEASAT-1 Altimetric Observations Study I authored for presentation in Toronto, Canada.

Spending time with my sister Annie (left) while visiting Ma Macy.

Research and Development was the priority now at Dahlgren. This was the new Warfare Analysis Department Building where much of my work was done.

Me and our first child Carolyn. I was enjoying Motherhood.

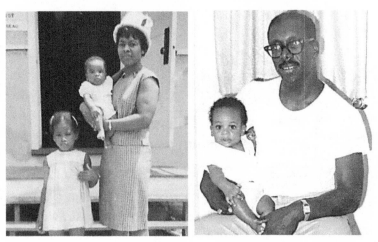

I enjoyed those days as a working mom, and Ira was an attentive dad.

Typical scene of Ira with the children when they were young.

Ira seemed to be good at everything including fatherhood.

Carolyn was busy with piano, swimming,
schoolwork, and fun time.

Our family all together. What a blessing to have each other.

Me with David and Carolyn.

Ira was breaking barriers too, as a black supervisor.

Another memorable moment with the children playing together.

My mathematical computations were now impacting groundbreaking satellite geodesy projects. Barriers were being broken.

My brother, Nolan, Jr. helped us clear our land.

Ira enjoyed the house building process.

The finished new house on ten acres in King George, Virginia. We are still here.

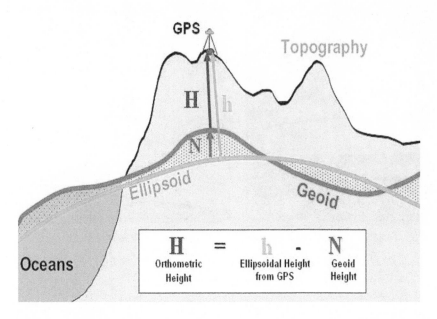

One of my duties was to calculate the geoid, the hypothetical shape of the earth, coinciding with mean sea level and its imagined extension under, or over land areas. Thus, it was more complicated if you were getting satellite data from over water, and that is where most of my work was done. (Text from Chapter 5) (table from GIS Stack Exchange)

CHAPTER SIX: GRATEFUL

We were enjoying the house in King George and feeling blessed as we had finally transitioned to living outside of the base. We had a short, ten-minute drive to the office. It took some getting used to in the beginning, but we adjusted well, especially since there was no rush hour traffic – Remember Dahlgren was in the country, or as some of you may humorously say... *in the sticks*. It was different for the children as well, as they were attending schools and involved in organizations in the King George community, as opposed to on the base. I was given more responsibility at work, being named project manager for another significant project, the 1978 SEASAT mission. It carried the first example of satellite-based synthetic aperture radar (SAR). SAR is now used for many civilian applications as well, such as subsidence monitoring for large-scale tunneling, and landslide studies and monitoring. I was also active in Toastmistress International, a world-wide organization whose mission is to train people in leadership roles, with the thought that this would help me land one of those supervisory positions within the organization. It was fun, challenging, and different. As a woman of color, I knew I had to be better than everyone else, which I felt would require very strong communication and leadership skills. What better way to develop those skills and abilities than to join Toastmistress International.

147

Carolyn was all grown up now and about to graduate from King George High School. It was hard to believe that little infant we loved, at first sight, was on her way to college. The graduation was low-key compared to some other graduations I had attended when I was coming up. It was a big deal to be graduating from high school back then for poor folks in the country, where there were no high expectations. Most of the students at King George High School were not only expected to graduate from high school, but also matriculate towards at least a college degree or more. Carolyn ranked towards the top of the class, so I was very happy that day. We knew the families of many of the other 100 or so graduates because most of them either lived on the base in the early years or worked there at Dahlgren. She had many friends who grew up in King George as well, so it was a fun occasion for her. Many of her high school classmates are still close friends with her today. The class had a party and Carolyn went for about an hour, then we celebrated together as a family. She had chosen Mary Washington College (now the University of Mary Washington), which is in nearby Fredericksburg, Virginia. I liked that she was going to be close by, and so did Ira. We were also pleased that she was such a role model for David and Michael, who were excited for her as well.

We were visiting Ma Macy more often, helping her with the house and with planting and harvesting in the garden. Carolyn was away at college most of the time, but the boys were older and helped us with a lot of the chores at Ma Macy's house. I was starting to notice that she was getting older, and her energy level and physical abilities were not what they had been before. Grandma Plum, Daddy's mom, was still living at the house and was well into her 100s. Carolyn always said she was a neat freak, but that slender, petite woman was just tough and very organized, in addition to being very smart. She used words like "entice" when I was a kid, and I had never heard an older person from the country speak words like that. Something else that was also memorable about Grandma Plum is that she wouldn't get dressed while the television was on. She always felt that somebody just may be looking back. What would she think about technology today? I think her real strength was her way of not worrying and not being stressed about things. She didn't let things worry her, which probably had a lot to do with her living so long. I know a lot of people who say they are stress-free, but my Grandma Plum lived that life every day. What a blessing it was for her to be living so long, and still wondering about strangers peeking at her unclothed body through that "tv box," as she called it. She was wonderful company for Ma Macy, and it was nice seeing them together, and learning as much about womanhood as I could from them.

Carolyn was enjoying everything about her college life. Mary Washington was more of an academic school, so if you were looking for parties and lots of socializing, it wasn't the school for you. She was majoring in Economics and had a high GPA. Before she graduated from high school, I was selected to the Dahlgren School Board, so she knew I was a stickler about academics, and that I was expecting her to do well in college. David was doing well and was about to graduate from high school soon, but Michael had some learning disabilities that kept him from excelling academically. However, he was the most athletic of the three kids and played high school basketball. Also, he was so much younger than Carolyn and did not have the benefit of her being around as a role model. We were so grateful that he was our baby boy, and we gave him all the help he needed. Around the beginning of Carolyn's college days, we lost our co-worker, friend, and the first black mathematician hired at Dahlgren. Herman Caster lost his battle with cancer, and we were heart-stricken, as he left behind his wife Marjorie and three children. He was the oldest and more experienced of all of us, and sort of the "Dean" of our group. All the black mathematicians and scientists who had been hired at Dahlgren over the years, even some who had left the base and accepted jobs at other agencies, were present at his home-going service, which was held on base at the Dahlgren Chapel. As much as we were going to miss Herman, I knew it would not amount to the loss his family was feeling, so we let them know they could count on us, and we prayed for them often.

David was a few months away from graduation when we got the call that Ma Macy had died. He cried that day, but no more than all of us as we huddled together by the fireplace reminiscing about our experiences with her, feeling grateful for the life she shared with us and somehow chuckling occasionally as well. Grandma Plum had just moved up north with one of her relatives. All those years of hard work had taken its toll on mama, and now she was gone. It felt like part of me was gone with her. We didn't look very much alike, but I was her daughter, no doubt about it. I had all her ways, values, and mannerisms. The only thing different was my formal education, which she would have earned too, if she had the opportunity. That old farm had seen a lot of ups and downs and struggles and heartache, and now Ma Macy, who was a joy to so many, had moved on to be with Daddy, and we were grieving once again. Ira seemed to love her as much as I did, and he said, "If there was ever anyone who made it to heaven, it was Ma Macy." I knew I was going to miss her, but like Ira said, "she was in a good place now." No more preparing for another cold winter, no more laboring for that tobacco factory, no more raising chickens, and working in the fields.

Everything was in order, just like when Daddy died. Ma Macy wouldn't have it any other way. Ira and I took care of all the arrangements with help from my sister Annie and my brothers, Joseph and Nolan, Jr. It was a bright sunny morning on the day of her service, and knowing Mama, she probably made that request to God in preparation for her home going. She was just always ahead of everything, you know. We didn't want her to go this soon, but Ma Macy was home now, relaxing with Daddy, looking down on us, and saying "Gladys Mae, don't let those young-ins mess up our house."

We were making sure all the business was being taken care of at the house in Sutherland and working on some important projects at Dahlgren at the same time. My 1981 technical paper *SEASAT Satellite Radar Altimetry Data Processing System*, outlined how radar altimetry data was combined with the Doppler precise orbits to correct atmospheric and environmental effects and tidal, ionospheric, tropospheric, and barometric data to produce improved geoid heights and vertical deflection data. The sea set mission lasted only 106 days because of electrical system issues, but good data was retrieved from the global array of ground-tracking stations. This work led to refinements in the critical mean-earth ellipsoid. This was one of two technical papers that I authored in 1981. They sure got their money's worth out of me that year, wouldn't you say? I had accomplished all that ground-breaking work for over a decade, balancing it with raising three children, earning my Master of Public Administration, and finding time to serve on the board of the Dahlgren Credit Union and the local school board. I didn't really think about it then, but now when I reflect, it's hard to believe I had all that stamina, commitment, and determination. I wanted to accomplish a lot in my life, more than others had before me, and after a little more than fifty years, I already had. I was so thankful, but I wasn't finished yet. The winter of 1982 was when Grandma Plum died peacefully and left behind her legacy. She was 111 years old. A centurion who had seen so many changes in the world. My paternal grandmother, Plum, was born five years after the Civil War ended and slavery was abolished. It's not hard to understand her toughness, her resiliency, her ability to survive through hard times. Her parents had been slaves, so they must have passed that resiliency on to her. She witnessed the onset of electricity, automation, automobiles, airplanes, telephones, computers, two world wars, a man walking on the moon, the world-wide-web, and her granddaughter working as a mathematician and playing a role in developing the GPS, which was used only by the government at that time. She also had been called colored, negro, black, African American, and some other names I'm sure that we won't mention. Now that's a lot of names – I should have asked her which she preferred before she left us, but then again, there are so many things I wish I could have asked her. From start to finish, what a life she must have lived. Now, how fascinating a memoir would that have been?

I continued to get recognized for my work at Dahlgren. I was writing quite a few other papers related to GPS, and was a project leader, but still there was something missing from my life. Despite all the professional accomplishments and educational achievements, I wanted more. Could it have been a higher supervisory position like the one held by Ira. He was supervising now and had been for several years. Even in the late 60s, he took on some team leader duties with the submarine-based missiles program, and one of the young black mathematicians that he helped train was a very bright young man out of Morehouse College named Herman Cain. He is the same fellow who went on to become a successful businessman, and who ran for the 2012 Republican Party nomination for President. That's just like Ira, mentoring younger guys back in the early days, and getting them to believe they can achieve anything. I would say his message sure did get through to Mr. Cain. Ira had earned his way to a supervisory position. That was still a white male-dominated role in the science and research industry, so it was a huge achievement in that environment, even for a black man like Ira. Our first black professional, Herman Caster, became the first black supervisor before Ira. I was so proud of my husband for what he had accomplished.

In 1983, a group of women in the King George and Fredericksburg, Virginia areas decided to form an alumni chapter of Alpha Kappa Alpha Sorority, Inc. I was among them, along with my Soror Pearl. I had not been active in my sorority since I graduated from Virginia State. This was most likely something that I needed in my life. Just when I thought something was missing, I had an opportunity to serve and give back to my community outside of the church, schools, and the workplace. Again, God made it possible for me to help others, and to cultivate new friendships again with some like-minded women who looked like me. There was plenty of work to do in building our new chapter in the beginning. Pearl and I were now charter members of our local chapter, Xi Upsilon Omega, and I served as chapter treasurer early on.

Carolyn graduated from Mary Washington with a B.S. in Economics and then earned her master's degree from Averett University. We were so proud of our baby girl, who was not a baby anymore. She had developed before our eyes and become a beautiful and charming woman. Our first grandchild, Andre, was born in 1986, and after a divorce, Carolyn raised him as a single mother, and Ira and I were the biggest supporters in her village.

I began to think more and more that God had sent me to Dahlgren, and it was no coincidence that Ira was already there. It was almost as if he was waiting on me to ride through those gates with my little brother Nolan, Jr. When you pray for his help and his guidance, sometimes that help comes indirectly or through other people he puts in your life to protect you, keep you safe, and give you encouragement as you experience challenges in your life, and oh, did I have many challenges. I often think about where I would be had Ira not been there. I am not sure if I would have adjusted so well to being away from home at that cold, sprawling military base, in the middle of winter, with very few people around who looked like me. They were not confronted with what I was experiencing as a woman of color, in the midst of a segregated, southern town, and having to prove every day that I could perform as well or better than my white (especially white male) colleagues.

Ira had been there more than two months before I started my career at Dahlgren, and he would be there until he retired in 1990, and it was always so comforting to know he was there with me, similarly situated and always having my back. It was a well-deserved retirement for him, after having to endure so much discrimination and still become a leader in a field in which very few black men had been successful, much less advanced to the supervisory level. He had served in the US Army during the Korean War and then contributed his mathematical and leadership skills to this nation as a civilian working at Dahlgren, where during his time as a Branch Head, he supervised the development of software systems in the fields of exterior ballistics, geo-ballistics, and anti-submarine warfare. I was there with him, by his side almost his entire career, so I was okay with him leaving before me, and as proud as a wife could be. By now, I was more than able to make it on my own. Now that he was retired, Ira was playing the grandfather role to the fullest and enjoying every minute of it.

We both spent quality time with our grandson Andre. Ira attended every ball game that he participated in, and I came out to the games as well. I was still working and couldn't quite imagine retiring because it just seemed like there was more to do and more to accomplish. When Andre started taking karate lessons, I signed up too. I also took piano lessons a couple years later since all the children were grown now and I didn't have as much to do when I wasn't at the office. The piano lessons were also another way to relax, and to challenge myself to learn something new, and to accomplish something I always wanted to do.

Ira always understood the benefits of relaxing better than I did. It quite possibly was something he picked up from his sports background, particularly his baseball days with the inning breaks and pitching changes. There's something often very calming about baseball. From chewing gum or sunflower seeds while your team is at bat, to raising the spirits of the clean-up batter from your seat in the dugout, to just turning around from your position in the field and taking in the summer breeze and the sculptured tree-lined landscape behind the outfield wall and feeling blessed for the experience. Now that's the way to relax, in his opinion. And as for the young sports fans of today, Ira doesn't agree with people wanting to change the rules to speed up the national pastime. He likes the game just the way it is, and he would possibly add an extra inning or two if it was up to him.

As much as he wanted to take a break after an early stint in the U.S. Army, and then serving those 35 years of dedicated service for our country at Dahlgren, Ira began to spend much needed time with Andre. I became attached to Andre as well. "Gammie" is what he would call me, and still does to this day. He was a blessing to us, and I quickly realized being in his life would not only benefit him, but also be a source of support and encouragement to Carolyn. She didn't date much while he was young, preferring to spend most of her time with Andre, and working on growing her career. My sons David and Michael also stepped up and helped a lot with Andre and seemed to love being uncles. They and Ira would attend all of Andre's youth baseball, basketball, and soccer games as he grew older. Even when the clock was down to the last few minutes or last innings, and it didn't look good for the home team, you could hear his uncles motivating words of encouragement, "Keep your head up Andre! If you keep fighting, there's always a chance." Those were my guys getting it done.

The World-Wide-Web, commonly known as the Web, an information system where documents and other web resources are identified by Uniform Resource Locators was launched, ushering in the Information Age. Released to the general public in late 1991, it could be accessed via the internet, which changed the world as we knew it. It eventually led to the creation of all things digital – Facebook, Twitter,

Instagram, and other platforms that keep us connected. The Web has been essential to the development of the information age and is the primary tool billions of us use to interact on the internet.

It was about this time that I decided to take a few classes that could possibly lead to a doctorate degree. Ira was behind me all the way because he knew that was one accomplishment I had always wanted, ever since we first discussed our life goals. I always imagined being like Dr. E. Louise Hunter, my mentor at Virginia State, who was the first black woman to earn a Ph.D. at the University of Virginia, as mentioned earlier. Dahlgren had a deal with Virginia Tech, like an extension of their campus, where we could take classes on base that would lead to graduate degrees. I took a few classes at a time, as I was still working full-time, and in my 60s by now. It was not easy, but I had a goal and was committed to it. I was working during the day, going to class, and studying in the evenings, and watching my Andre grow up whenever I could. We were also still enjoying riding down to the country most weekends, and little Andre, who was not so little anymore, was tagging along with us.

Although I had produced some impactful work regarding GPS, and several important papers, there were many times after entering the Ph.D. program when I was amazed at just how smart I was. One occasion, that really stands out, took me by surprise. It was when a group of us from the class decided to drive up together to the Virginia Tech main campus in Blacksburg to meet with our professors and, more importantly, prepare for a big exam. During the study group sessions, we were all supposed to go through the possible questions and share the answers with one another. After about an hour or so, I realized that most of the questions were being answered by me. Naturally, since everyone else in the group was white and I was the only woman, I'm thinking these guys are showing their true colors. They are not sharing answers with me because they are prejudiced and do not want to see a black woman succeed. I thought *here we go again.* I was wrong, though. Those guys were not holding back, they just didn't know the answers. They were relying on me to give them the answers and solve the problems. I think I helped a lot of white men pass that class and stay eligible for their PhDs that week.

Then there was a fellow in my classes who was from the deep south somewhere, I suppose Mississippi or Alabama, and he sounded the part. He was an engineer at the base, and when I first met him, it was obvious he had very little exposure to black people who were on his academic and career level. He seemed so uncomfortable, and I thought, "I'm the one who should be uncomfortable," with me being the only black woman in this Ph.D. program. His only exposure to black folks was with the ones who worked for his daddy back home. His family had a nice size farming business and a little store down south, and the only black people he really knew were the ones working for them in the fields and in the house doing domestic work.

After some time in the program, he finally got the nerve to speak to me, study with me, and finally worked his way up to having lunch with me and my husband Ira. During that lunch, he apologetically told us that his parents treated blacks poorly and felt they were inferior and were not very bright. He confessed, almost religiously, that his beliefs had been the same as his parents when he was a kid because of his parents' conditioning, and that's all he knew. They had kept him away from blacks, and his schools were basically all white. He realized that he had been totally wrong after being around us and the other black professionals on the base. He also complemented us on our character, professionalism, and intelligence. We were almost speechless as we finished what was left of our sandwiches and ice teas because we never thought it could be possible that someone like him would ever change. We learned an important lesson that day. That experience taught us that you never give up on a person because sometimes people change as a result of their life experiences or people they come in contact with, and in this case, it was clearly a change for the better. He is an example of someone who changed his bigotry towards a group of people because he allowed himself to get to know them for who they really are. That fellow and I were friends now, and we would both move on in the Ph.D. program successfully. I was proud of him and proud of how Ira and I helped him become a better person. He's no longer with us, but I'm sure he's looking down from heaven on us now, instead of looking up.

As I mentioned in the introduction, when I received the call from my professor informing me that I passed the competencies with flying colors, I was ecstatic beyond words. I was not only happy for myself, but for all my family, especially those who were no longer with us. I was thanking God for giving me the strength and will to make my dream a reality. Now I had to write the dissertation, and I would be able to walk across that stage. I had waited a long time for this, and I was not going to let a paper get in the way of my dream. I wanted to take a break first. I was exhausted, and I wanted to take some time to decide on the topic of my dissertation. After some careful thought, I decided to retire from my position at Dahlgren. It was time, and I remember the big smile on Ira's face as he agreed. The retirement party was attended by a medium-sized group of colleagues, former co-workers, friends, and our family came too. It was a good day and a proud day for me, celebrating 42 years of service to my country. Several colleagues spoke, and I remember words that stood out: *dedication, commitment, dependable, respected, smart.* If I didn't know any better, I would say they all had Ma Macy write those speeches as those were the exact words she always used to describe me. She would have been proud beyond those words.

I started to work a little on my dissertation, so I could get Ma Macy to smile down on me at my doctoral graduation. This is also the period of time where we decided to travel and check off another place on our bucket list. Besides, I deserved it after 42 years of *dedicated service.* I had traveled to our satellite station in Guam for work purposes, which was quite an exciting journey. We had also visited Europe and the Caribbean before with a travel group, mostly made up of current or former Dahlgren employees. The group was planning a trip to another part of the world that we had not yet traveled. The itinerary, which started with a flight to New Zealand, and included cruising to Australia, aroused my curiosity. Before we knew it, we were on our flight, heading to New Zealand.

I had always liked flying, but my flight to New Zealand opened my eyes to what was beneath all those beautiful clouds as I looked out below the aircraft from my window seat. The clouds had always been visible on flights, but this time they were more intriguing and had me reflecting on all the computations I had performed to calculate the shape of the Earth for the many projects I was assigned to. It made me think of a quote that I had heard from one of America's greatest writers, Thomas Wolfe, who said – "I have to see a thing a thousand times before I see it once." I started to realize how important that work was, and how blessed I was to have an opportunity to be a part of something so big, so impactful. We see clouds all the time, and usually, we don't like to see them when we look up into the sky, but from more than 30,000 feet above the ocean, those clouds had a different meaning for me that day, and oh what a glorious view it was. Quite often, it is a normal thing not to notice something that is always there, so we take it for granted. Likewise, things appear a lot different, and much more interesting when you look at them from a slightly different perspective. I was feeling thankful and appreciative for this moment, and for what we normally consider the little things.

After a long but comfortable flight, we were eager to discover this remotely located country. New Zealand is known for its picturesque landscape and what a beautiful place it was. Matter of fact, it was like nowhere that we had been before. I enjoyed learning about its indigenous Maori culture, and Ira became aware of some of the players on its world-famous national rugby team. Soon we were on the cruise ship and off to Australia. Unfortunately, there were some very bad storms in the South Pacific at the time, which made for an uncomfortable trip on the sea at times. I don't think I ever got my sea legs that trip, but I did enjoy the Australian ports, especially Melbourne, in the southeastern part of the mainland, with its wonderful museums and multicultural themes. Sydney was also a favorite with both of us. It's the country's largest city, with a magnificent harbor and beautiful beaches. With much to discover, and a good pair of sneakers, we were good to go. We enjoyed our time away on this journey. We spent so much time volunteering and doing for others, so this was just what we needed. Time to rest, explore, and spend time together with no alarm clocks and meetings to attend. It was just the two of us, something we could use a lot more of moving forward.

We returned home with lots of souvenirs and memories to last for the rest of our lives. I sat back and relaxed and put my feet up when I got back to Virginia, to rest a little as I had never been away on a vacation that long. After a week or two, I realized I still had a paper to write; I was committed to finishing my doctoral dissertation. A few weeks after returning, I began experiencing vertigo. Then I attended the funeral of a close friend and co-worker, Carol Ann Malyevac, and six days later, I had a massive stroke. It was Thursday, May 28, 1998, and I will always remember it as the day my life radically changed, at least for the moment. I thought I would be working on that dissertation. However, the almighty apparently had other plans for my life at that point because suddenly, my world went into a rapid spin. I screamed to my husband for help, and he called for an ambulance and comforted me until it arrived. After a series of preliminary tests and finally being admitted to the hospital, I surmised from the reactions of the medical staff, that I was very sick.

I was put in the intensive care unit, and by the end of the first week, the doctors determined that I had two strokes. After I thought about it, I had been having symptoms of this illness such as double vision, and weakness on my right side, but didn't think seriously about it. After all, the idea of a stroke was so foreign to me. I thought I was too young and healthy for anything like that to happen to me. I felt trapped, but I immediately committed myself to face the challenge head on and recover as quickly as possible. I wanted to maximize the capabilities that I had left, which meant hard, painstaking work, and a positive mental approach. During the three-week period of hospitalization and rehabilitation, I searched for the meaning of this new and devastating experience. After some deep spiritual introspection, I realized the importance of several things in my life. This included things like family, spending more time on myself, finding my true purpose, living, and enjoying each day to the fullest, as well as sharing my wisdom and knowledge with others and seeing the big picture.

This period of my life also gave me an opportunity to observe others, especially those who had conditions more challenging than mine. This motivated me to count my blessings and appreciate how fortunate I was that therapy could restore much of what I had lost from the illness. Yes, I had to face the new me and my limitations, but I knew with faith, I would be ok. I could not wait to return to my home as I knew it would give me so much comfort and pleasure. It was Summer by the time I returned home, and the house that I called home was a wonderful sight to see. As Ira made the sharp left turn onto our long, winding, tree-lined driveway, I noticed all the beautiful flowers, the perfectly cut grass, and the singing birds now more than ever before.

I felt energized now that I was home. Soon I began attending a therapy program and met some new friends who had similar problems with mobility and speech. There was a tremendous boost to my mindset as a result of the social connection with others who were just as determined as me. Coupled with Ira being there getting me back on my feet, one leg and one day at a time, this helped me maintain my drive and positive attitude. Ira was just as important as that portable walker that I was holding onto daily as I pushed myself first from the bedroom to the kitchen and then up and eventually down that long driveway that leads to the main road. Ira was there with me, each difficult step of the way, with his steady, helpful, and calm demeanor. I did wonder "why me" occasionally, but I never felt sorry for myself.

Two months after the stroke, I was back attending church and other activities in a limited capacity. My physical endurance determined the kind of work-rest routine I had to develop. I was so grateful for, and appreciated all the available assistive devices and equipment, but my goal was to rid myself of them as soon as possible. After I completed my therapy program in February 1999, I quickly enrolled in a regular fitness program that I attended four days a week. Nine months after my stroke, I was focused completely on exercise, reading, and crossword puzzles. Then I worked my way up to daily walks, and gradually increased my distance until I reached 2.4 miles. This inspired me to participate in a local 3.1-mile walk. I successfully completed it in less than 55 minutes. To quote my favorite Bible verse, "I can do all things through Christ which strengthens me." I live by that quote, but it doesn't hurt to have a best friend like Ira West as well. Here again, Ira was the right man for the job. Some say don't chase people; just work hard, be a good example, and be yourself. The people who belong in your life will come and find you, and they will stay there. He found me in that blue pleated skirt, my first week at Dahlgren, and he has always been there for me – as if someone had written him into my life script.

Another year had come and gone, but this was no ordinary year. This new year was supposed to be unpredictable as we were moving from 1999 and into the 21st century. People were predicting all sorts of things happening, like clocks stopping and, of course, computers malfunctioning. It was quite entertaining to watch mostly young folks running around *like roosters with their heads cut off*, as Ma Macy would say.

Those last days before the new year came in, Ira and I felt like just sitting in front of the television with a bowl of popcorn, and just looking at all the commotion of the news stations reporting on these theories of what might happen and so forth. We chuckled to ourselves because we realized these folks had not seen all the depressions, wars, assassinations, segregation, and civil unrest that we had seen. You see, no matter what happened in the past, the world always continued to turn, and the clocks kept ticking. In my mind, that number 2000 would come in just like every year had done before it. The new year came in and I smiled to myself, thinking, "I told you so." Ira and I didn't have the popcorn as I suggested previously, but we did have a little comfort food and the company of our family beside us on New Year's Day as we celebrated another new year for the planet Earth.

The next thing I knew, I was slowly but surely working toward completing my dissertation. It was not that difficult, but it took a lot of my time away from my family, and after the stroke, I cherished every minute with them. I just stayed focused though and soon it was completed. Ira was so happy I had finished the paper because he wanted us to do more things together again now that the dissertation was done, and my health appeared to be back to normal. I graduated with a Ph.D. in public administration and public affairs in May 2000. It took some hard work, but I did it. My daddy, my mama, and Drs. John and Louise Hunter would have been proud of this country girl if they were still here to witness it. Although, if you ask me, I think they just may have received the news somehow. I couldn't stop smiling on that graduation day, realizing it was the most amazing accomplishment of my life. Don't get me wrong, my contribution to the success of the GPS gives me chills just to think about it, even today, but it was me just doing my job as I said before. It wasn't something that I dreamed of accomplishing all my adult life, and I never realized it would have such an impact in the world. The Ph.D. behind my name was a personal goal, a challenge I was committed to. I never gave up – I stayed the course as I had done so many times before and would continue to do in the future.

However, while taking some planned tests at my doctor's office as a follow-up to the stroke, the doctor found that I had coronary artery blockages. It would require quadruple bypass surgery to correct the problem. The good news was that there had been recent advances in heart surgery by that time, so it wasn't as risky as we thought at first. The recovery time would be about 8 weeks, as far as regular walking, and walking up and down stairs. The surgery was a success. I had some brief aches and pains for a few weeks afterward, but I made a full recovery within a couple months and was back on my feet again, just like the doctor predicted I would be. I could pretty much live a normal life again, with proper attention to my diet and exercise patterns. Ira and my children were there for me again, giving me encouragement and keeping me in good spirits. David and his new wife, and Andre, who was now in high school, were all giving me hugs and attention, now more than ever. Even Michael, who was not in the area at the time, was showing me love. I let them know they could count on me being around for a while.

America was still reeling from the devastating 9/11 terrorist attacks on the World Trade Center and the Pentagon just a couple months prior to my surgery. It was the worst and most shocking thing I had experienced since the attacks on Pearl Harbor by Japan when I was a young girl. *Could America bounce back again, and were we still able to get past such disasters?* I thought to myself. I was also asking similar questions about myself. I had been through a lot of adversity and this was just another situation where I would have to recycle the good times, and I did. My good days always outweighed my bad days, thanks to the good Lord. He was with me again.

Gideons International is a worldwide organization with the purpose of bringing others to a saving knowledge of our Lord and Savior, Jesus Christ. We joined the King George, Virginia Camp in 2001, and devoted ourselves to its mission. I was thanking God every day for the simple things in life and feeling grateful that I was still alive and given more time on this earth to contribute to my family, and to others, in any way I could. After years of tough life experiences, I sometimes had a difficult time falling off to sleep at night. My faith and knowledge of the Lord would always keep me strong, though, and I also relaxed by thinking back to my imaginative days growing up in Sutherland – listening to the rhythmic sounds of the raindrops on that old tin roof, and how safe and wonderful it made me feel. The appreciation of little things like that can be important in life and keep one grounded and grateful.

Dr. Gladys B. West

I spoke briefly at my retirement dinner about my 42 years
of service. The dinner was held in Fredericksburg, Virginia.

We traveled to Australia and New Zealand after my retirement.

What a wonderful evening as we celebrated my PH.D graduation.

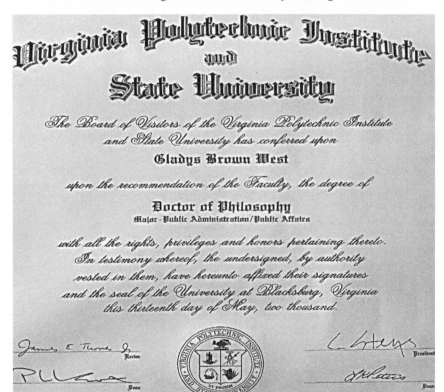

Born just after the Civil War, Grandma Plum was going on 112 years old when she passed on. Long enough to see me play an integral role in the development of the GPS. I think she was satisfied.

CHAPTER SEVEN: THE JOURNEY CONTINUES

I have always felt strongly about voting in local and national elections, and at times, Ira and I have volunteered for some local candidates, especially after retirement. Since we had to fight so hard to get the right to vote as black Americans, it was our belief that voting should be taken seriously. Ira's brother, Roy, who was originally an educator, became Mayor of Richmond, Virginia, in 1982, back when the city council members selected the Mayor from within their ranks. That was a story itself considering how poor they were growing up. When Barack Obama threw his hat into a crowded group of hopefuls for the Democratic presidential nomination, I was not surprised, but I did not give him much of a chance, despite my instinct to immediately make him my favorite. My dreams for a black man or woman to be nominated by a party to become the United States President always seemed out of reach; thinking of him literally winning the general election seemed quite impossible. I thought the U.S. Senator from Illinois was way ahead of his time and that this may not be the right time for him to be a legitimate candidate.

Boy was I wrong. President Obama won that race convincingly in 2008 and changed the face of American politics. My mouth hung open for several days. After all I had experienced growing up in segregation, being one of the "first" to integrate the professional staff at Dahlgren,

173

and being discriminated against for so many years, there was a black family in the White House, and the impact was unbelievable. President Obama was smart, well educated, an eloquent speaker, and oh by the way, a wonderful father and husband. It was almost too good to be true. Just listening to him speak, I noticed that his beliefs represented some of Ma Macy's teachings – commitment, honesty, and steadfastness. He was a positive role model for the young people of our country. He was a breath of fresh air in so many ways as he gained the support of many underserved groups across the nation, especially people of color. Another of my dreams was reached in a way because I never thought I would see a black president in my lifetime.

Things were changing so much now as technology was advancing rapidly in our society. The GPS was being used in many ways now, in every industry. It was all quite amazing to me, although I am still known to pull out a map occasionally. Ira is guilty as well, but not as much as I am. I'm just old school, I presume. My family was ever changing as well during this time. I enjoyed seeing Andre now as he had grown into the man that I knew he would. He was a college graduate. Carolyn was married again, and we were very happy for her. Michael and Lisa's boys were growing up fast, and David and his wife, Colleen, have two adult children and one son in high school now. It seemed like just yesterday, we were holding our children in our arms and preparing them for the world, and now they were all doing the same for our grandchildren, and it was a joy to see. I was especially enjoying when we all got together on holidays, and of course our annual family reunions that were bigger and better than ever every Summer in North Dinwiddie. It was also interesting during this time to observe how our country was responding to having a black President. There were so many who obviously wanted him to fail, but he remained steadfast, did some wonderful things, and inspired so many of our youth.

A little over halfway through Obama's first term, my doctor discovered that I had breast cancer. *Not again* is what I was thinking, but at the same time I had faith, and I knew God would be with me as he had been before. There was just too much left for me to accomplish in this life, and I prayed for strength once again. I had surgery to remove a tumor, then it was radiation at the Stafford Cancer Center five days a week for six weeks. Emotionally, I was strong. I was shaken at first, but then I reflected on the life I had lived, and all that God had done for me, so I held my head up high and kept going. A quote by Maya Angelou came to my mind, "*The more you know of your history, the more liberated you become.*" I knew my history was that of a survivor, and a descendant of some very strong women, and that was all the confidence and liberation I needed. I remember enjoying having something as little as a package of cookies after treatments. Those cookies made me smile and made me feel like I was getting better with every treatment. The most memorable occurrence was that I still attended our family reunion that year, and then had my last radiation treatment the following Monday. You know I had lots of cheerleaders that weekend at the reunion. My daughter Carolyn came to meet me at the treatment center on that last day to celebrate with Ira and me. When I saw them, I said, "God is good," and they both responded, "All the time."

God seems to always be there for me, but that would not be possible if I did not have faith and put my trust in him. Even when I was a young girl, I put my trust in God and he always seemed to show me the way. I am often asked why I was chosen by the Hunters at Virginia State when they were looking for someone to help them in their home. After giving it much thought over the years, and thanking God for blessing me with that experience, I have a good feeling now that it was no coincidence. I apparently had made a very good impression on the faculty during my first year at Virginia State, without knowing it. The Hunters must have observed that I had that strong work ethic, values, and character, which by the way, had been instilled in me by Ma Macy. It finally came to me that they may have handpicked me because they saw in me what my parents had been bragging about all along. While they realized my guileless nature and trusted me to be a good example for their daughter, it was the man upstairs who put me there at the right time to make it happen.

As I have mentioned earlier, I am a proud member of Alpha Kappa Alpha Sorority, Inc. (AKA), which by the way, is the sorority of which my mentor, Dr. E. Louise Hunter, was a lifetime member. The late Katherine Johnson, a mathematician featured in the book and motion picture, *Hidden Figures,* was also an AKA. I guess there is something about an AKA woman, right. I was not as active with the sorority when I first started out in my career, nor in my early days of marriage and motherhood. In the 1980s, I became active again, reaching back in any way I could to the young sisters of the Pink and Green, and assisting with community service activities that we are known for. My daughter Carolyn also decided to follow me and became a legacy member of the sorority and is very active with our chapter. I had always been involved in activities throughout my career. After my quadruple bypass surgery, I discontinued my piano lessons, so I had extra time to work with my sorority. I was still active with my Isshinryu Karate lessons, but to a lesser degree. I rose to the level of Green Belt. Ira and I were very consistent with our exercise classes at the YMCA, and we still are. Sometimes I go in there and exercise with those young girls. They have youth on their side, but I hang in there with them and at least go through the motions. I am getting older, but I still need activities to challenge my mind and satisfy my need to learn. We even participate in a lot of the community and social events and activities there as well.

After retirement, I did not continue with Toastmistress, which I had got involved in mid-career. I even served as President of our Toastmistress International chapter one year. Now, we were taking on leadership roles in Gideons International. It is an association of Christian business and professional men and their wives dedicated to telling people about Jesus. The more we became involved with this wonderful group of people, the closer we became to Jesus. We get together for service and to share our personal testimony, and we are most known for providing Bibles and New Testaments to hotels, motels, hospitals, and shelters. With 63 years of marriage together, this has been something that has helped to strengthen that bond even more as we stand together in faith and will continue it in the future.

I have remained very active with my sorority, Alpha Kappa Alpha (AKA). A few years ago, the senior members of our chapter were being honored at one of the meetings. When they introduced me, my introduction included information about my retirement after 42 years at Dahlgren and that I had worked on the Global Positioning System. My Soror, Gwen James, said her antenna went up immediately. She spoke with me after the meeting and got my story. She asked my daughter and me if she could take the information to a reporter. We said, "why not, if you think people would be interested." Gwen said she did not understand why anyone would not be interested, given the significance of what I had accomplished since there is no segment of our global society that does not utilize this technology. She went on to say that too many people of color in my generation, and before, never received the proper credit in history for their contributions, especially in technology and the sciences. Gwen is also a member of my Virginia State alumni chapter, and she couldn't believe that she was just hearing about my contributions after all the years she had known me. I told her I was just doing my job and never looked for any recognition. She pointed out that my work and recognition went farther than Dahlgren and the Navy. Gwen said, "You should be recognized for your work on GPS because of the impact it has made on the world. Little girls of color need to see you and know about you." Soon after, Gwen wrote an article about me for our sorority newsletter and took it to a local newspaper reporter. The next thing I knew, I was featured in the local newspaper.

Things really picked up from there. I had volunteered to speak to groups of young students before, but now I was being asked to do so many more events. I especially liked speaking to little girls, to get them to realize, if I could do it in 1956, then they could surely do it now. All they have to do is reach out and touch it. I began speaking to children at schools throughout the region, from Dahlgren, Virginia to Fort Washington, Maryland, telling my story and hoping to get at least one boy or girl to begin with a dream, and then put in the work to create their own success story. Mentoring children has become a passion of mine as I continue this journey.

Sometimes in life, you must get through the storms and the rain. You see me now, and you see a happy, successful person, but don't think that I haven't struggled or dealt with adversity. The real story shows the actual life experiences I have gone through. I don't cry about it though. I choose to smile. At the end of the day, those experiences made me stronger and more of an example to others. In this life that has been more like an adventure, I choose to feel blessed, be positive and keep smiling, because although I have a vast imagination, I never thought I would contribute to developments with tremendous scientific and societal impacts. Some call it "black girl magic," and I like the term, especially as a builder of self-esteem, but there is no magic in being the best at what you do. The magic, if you will, is that you are smart, beautiful and have the ability to achieve anything if you work hard and dedicate yourself to a particular goal. No magic can get you through a tough mathematics examination or help you pass a bar exam if you don't study for it. It takes preparation, commitment, determination, and prayer to achieve your goals. My message to those coming behind me is to let God be your magic and your source of strength. Then combine that with a strong work ethic and a commitment to make our world a better place. I learned that from my parents. My mother and father are the roots and trees that I came from. Therefore, any good deeds or accomplishments that I make happen, or any change in the world that I am part of – it is them who made it possible. Their strong example as parents made it all attainable. That is the magic they provided me… if only they could see how I have been honored and recognized in the last few years.

"Always keep some room in your heart for the unimaginable." That was a quote by the late Pulitzer Prize winning American poet, Mary

Oliver. I always lived by quotes like that and wondered what might come next in life. However, after that article by my AKA sorority sister, it seemed requests for me were coming in from everywhere. A few years earlier, I never would have imagined all this attention I was getting. I was almost feeling like Beyoncé – well maybe not quite, but you know what I mean. I was being recognized by so many media outlets, newspapers, magazines, radio show interviews, and even television shows like the 700 Club. I am also being featured in a documentary, *Women of Color in STEM*, which profiles some remarkable women, and addresses the under-representation of Women of Color in mathematics, technology, engineering, and the sciences. Later, I was profiled on ABCs "The View" during Black History Month, and this year AARP featured several individuals of color on their website and online newsletter who had made contributions to society, and I was one of them. The "unimaginable" was now very much a reality.

Although we developed the GPS at Navy, the Air Force operates the system and its satellites now. In late 2018, I was inducted into the Air Force Space and Missile Pioneers Hall of Fame in a big ceremony at the Pentagon Building. The little girl from the country with all those big dreams had never imagined anything like this. I was as excited with all of this as I was when I was notified that I had passed my doctoral competencies. You see, I was the first Woman of Color to be inducted into this prestigious group who had served this country to the highest of standards. I would now be among them in the annals of Air Force history. I was proud for my family and me, that day, as I walked into that building with Ira, our children, and our grandchildren at our sides. I thought I would be a little nervous sitting before so many guests and well-wishers in the audience, but for some reason, I was not. Maybe that was the re-laxed, calm nature of Grandma Plum coming out in me. Many of the onlookers were servicemen and women who wanted to see this little lady who contributed to something that was now a part of their everyday life, though others, especially women of color, were there to get a glimpse of a woman who looked like them, who in their words had the courage and commitment to pave the way for them to become contributors and offic-ers in the U.S. military. From my vantage point, it was a thing of beauty to see them in their uniforms and various skin tones and colors out in that audience, but I did not tear up. As a matter of fact, it seemed almost everyone shed a tear or two, except for me. I kept thinking about all the women before me who had not had this opportunity. I and those women of color seated before me in all their excellence represented "our ances-tors' wildest dreams," as penned by the great Maya Angelou. General Stayce Harris, the first black woman to rise to the rank of "Three Star General" in the United States Air Force, was particularly recognizable as she led an emotional standing ovation from the front row of the room. She later thanked me for opening doors and inspiring black women like herself to think and dream big. She is retired now, after serving our coun-try so honorably. Little did she know, I was just as honored to meet her. I couldn't help but think, perhaps General Harris will be the next woman of color inducted into this Hall of Fame. She has my vote.

My alma mater, Virginia State University (VSU), honored me around the same time by selecting me to be the Grand Marshal of the Homecoming Parade. I rode in style that day, just ahead of the royal court, as the band marched ahead of us. As a mathematician, I was ex-pecting instructions on how to be a grand marshal, but there were none.

My job was just to wave to the crowd, smile, and just look important. I'm sure I got at least two of those three things right. One of my fondest memories of that day was getting to meet the VSU President, Dr. Makola Abdullah. He was so kind and expressed that he was extremely honored to meet me. I was probably just as honored to meet him. I let him know that I was very pleased with what he was doing with my Alma Mater and that I liked the changes that were being made on the campus. We laughed and joked about so many things that day, but I will always remember what he said to me. He said, "For the students, it's so important for them to know that they can reach fantastic places from the seats they are sitting in today." He followed with, "They (students) don't really get it until they have someone come back and say I used to sit where you are sitting, and I helped to create something that changed the world…you don't have to come from somewhere else to do great things, you can come from Virginia State." It takes a message like that one from Dr. Abdullah to realize how important you are to others, and how you can inspire young people without knowing it. As an HBCU graduate himself (Howard University), he feels that schools like VSU do not guarantee success but gives access and opportunity to that success if a young person is willing to do the work that it takes to be successful. I could not agree more. As I rode along the parade route and into the stadium area, I got a warm feeling from the applause we received. I thought about those words he had just spoken to me, and it felt good. I was proud to know that my accomplishments were meaningful to so many young people. Hopefully, some young person may have been motivated to chase his or her dream a little harder after that day. The next time I was Grand Marshal of a parade was when Ira and I rode together as a couple in the King George Fall Festival

Parade. I didn't need any instructions this time. I was a veteran at Marshaling now, and Ira just followed my lead. If anyone is ever looking for a veteran Grand Marshal, we have the experience, that's if we aren't too busy.

Another big moment in this continuing journey came when I was honored at the 7th Annual Strong Men & Women in Virginia History program last year, and it was an evening that I will never forget. Held at the Richmond Marriott, the program honors prominent African Americans past and present who have made noteworthy and admirable contributions to the commonwealth, the nation, and to their professions. I was honored along with many who have persevered through struggles and challenges to become members of the armed forces, authors, community leaders, educators, judges, and politicians. People who serve their communities. The Library of Virginia and Dominion Energy have partnered for several years to make this program possible, and I am so grateful for their commitment to celebrating the achievements of people of color, who historically have been overlooked. During the ceremony, Librarian of Virginia, Sandra G. Treadway, so eloquently stated, "The life stories and accomplishments of the men and women honored this year are powerful and inspirational, and it is wonderful to have this opportunity to share their contributions with a wide audience." Her words touched my heart and had me reflecting on how far I had come in this life. Suddenly, I had a good feeling that I had taken that right path. The road I had often dreamed about as a child had led me to this place, and now I was being honored by the same commonwealth that had once lawfully restricted my rights as a citizen through segregation and old Jim Crow. The state that had looked down on me was now looking up at me, or at least looking me in the eye and saying, "Thank you for your strong character, your contributions, your job well done – thanks for never giving up on us...we are finally beginning to get it right." That's what my heart was hearing from the Commonwealth of Virginia that seasonably cold February night in Richmond, Virginia. My children were there supporting me as always, as well as some nieces and nephews. I particularly noticed my grandson Andre as he helped his "Gammie" from the stage at the end of the ceremony. He had been married to his wife Lia for only a few months at the time. I was glad to make them proud. I announced that night that I was donating my award money to Virginia State University. There were a few cheers and notable applause from the guests, some probably Virginia State alumni, and some who could have felt from my speech that it was my way of giving back to the place where it all started for me.

So many honors have come my way in the last few years, and another recognition that was especially heartfelt was when Dinwiddie County, the place where I was born and raised, honored me. The county Board of Supervisors recognized me during their monthly board meeting at the Dinwiddie Government Center with a resolution in my name that will remain eternally in the minutes at the county administration building. It was a time to celebrate this hometown girl for my *faith, ambition, mathematical talent, and valuable contribution to the development of the Global Positioning System*, as many of my family and friends were present. There were also some high school alumni members, representatives from the VSU Dinwiddie Alumni Chapter, and sorority sisters on hand to support me. The Delta Omega Chapter of AKA was the organization that nominated me for this recognition. I found it especially gratifying because it is the AKA chapter that my mentor Dr. Louise Hunter was a founding member of in its infancy. I kept thinking she must be dancing and smiling down on me this evening. It certainly conjured up some memories of lessons I learned from her. Earlier in the day, I thought about the first time she introduced me to the women of Delta Omega Chapter and challenged me to follow their example in service to others and commitment to excellence. I realized I had become the woman that she envisioned I could be when she took me under her wings many years ago. I was no longer Gladys Mae, the little country girl with tons of potential; I was Dr. Gladys West now, and I owed a tremendous amount of that success to Louise Hunter. I believe she was with me in spirit all evening, nodding her approval.

It was my special day, and I don't think I stopped smiling for the entire evening. VSU President, Dr. Abdullah, was kind enough to be in attendance as well. He was running late for the event, and when he arrived, he spoke to the audience with these comments, "Ironically, I would not have been able to make it to the event without Dr. West. I wasn't sure of the location, so I used my GPS to get here. Without her hard work, I literally may not have gotten to the event." It made everyone think for a split second, and then there was laughter and applause. He pulled me aside that evening and warmly thanked me for including him and Virginia State whenever I am recognized for my achievements. He said it is like "tying my brand to Virginia State University, which is more than enough by itself, but the monetary gifts that I have made to the university is an even more beautiful thing." Then he leaned in and said he is a fan of mine. The same man who was voted HBCU Male President of the Year a couple years ago admiring me – now how do you like that?

When Dr. Abdullah was hired to be VSU's 14th president, he said, "I believe in God. I believe in family. I believe in the transformative nature of education. I believe in Virginia State University." Since then, both of his children have graduated from HBCUs, with his daughter graduating Summa Cum Laude from Virginia State during the Winter Commencement of 2018, at the age of 19. He gave his daughter a big hug and kiss as she walked across the stage, and the commencement speaker that day was Deshauna Barber, Miss USA 2016, a Virginia State Alumnus. I admire a person who backs up what he or she believes, and it is refreshing to have him leading the way and setting a solid example for our young people today. At the end of the evening in Dinwiddie, my first thought was that Dr. Abdullah was such a kind man for driving down to the country to be there for me, but it was his words that truly resonated with me that night. It was an unforgettable event, and I had fun sipping punch, snacking on desserts, and having some great conversation with my friends, family, and President Abdullah and his wife, Ahkinyala.

Soon after that event, I was notified that Dr. Abdullah had nominated me to represent Virginia State University in the National Black College Alumni Hall of Fame Foundation (NBCA HOF). It is an organization dedicated to the growth and development of HBCUs through scholarships, internships, training and technical assistance, and alumni recognition for their service, contributions, and humanitarian efforts. I was selected to be among this esteemed group of men and women and inducted into the Hall of Fame in Atlanta, Georgia, which is where the NBCA is located. I knew it was a special honor once I was selected, but after arriving in Atlanta and seeing the names and pictures of the other individuals who had been inducted since the Hall of Fame was founded, it felt like I was having the most wonderful dream, except it was real. My name was now listed along with notables like Leontyne Price (Central State), Lionel Richie (Tuskegee), Phylicia Rashad (Howard), Debbie Allen (Howard), Eddie Robinson (Grambling State), Walter Payton (Jackson State), Earl Monroe (Winston Salem State), Oprah Winfrey (Tennessee State), Thurgood Marshall (Lincoln of Pennsylvania and Howard), John Lewis (Fisk), Katherine Johnson (West Virginia State) and Dr. Martin Luther King, Jr. (Morehouse). Is that a dream team or what? If you ever go to the website, check out the over 300 Hall of Fame members of this wonderful organization that is supporting and preserving our HBCUs, and you just might see Nolan and Macy Brown's daughter listed there too – as of this writing, I'm the last name listed in the Science category.

Another of my favorites last year was when the Fulton Bank and Fahrenheit Advisors sponsored an incredibly special Black History Month tribute to me for my work on the GPS project. I was asked to speak to the gathering of people who were there to meet me and recognize my body of work. I shared my story with them and afterward I was presented with a portrait by artist Jerome Jones. He is a renowned artist who along with his son Jeromyah have painted many other portraits of notable black Americans. Ira's first cousin, Linda Milton was one of the organizers of the event. Great work cousin Linda, and the portrait is lovely.

Then came a lovely evening at the Virginia Museum of History and Culture that I shared with Margot Lee Shetterly, author of the bestseller, *Hidden Figures*. There was an exhibit featuring my work in the upstairs of the museum that my family enjoyed observing, and that was fascinating for me as well. It was an evening that included a reception with refreshments, a presentation by Margot, telling the story of how she was able to write her book, and then a sit-down Q and A session with the two of us on stage responding to questions before a sellout crowd in the Museum's massive auditorium. Margot and I were so comfortable together, as we sat there in a rather cozy setting with a coffee table flanked by two high backed Queen Anne chairs. The spotlight was on us that night, as she talked about those wonderful ladies at NASA and her connection with them, and I fielded questions about the GPS and questions regarding being one of the first women of color hired as a mathematician at Dahlgren. The setting eventually moved to the main rotunda of the building as Margot and I sat side by side again at a table to meet and greet the patrons, who had formed lines halfway to the front door. Nobody was trying to leave before meeting us it seemed, and it was alright with us. We took selfies with them, signed autographs, and got to know a little about those folks. I got a little tired towards the end of the event, but I hung in there until I shook the hand of the last person in line. Besides, I knew I could sleep on the way home that night. Ira and I were in good hands on that peaceful ride back to King George with Carolyn and her husband Barry at the wheel, as they had done so many times before.

After all the acknowledgments and recognition that I have recently received, the following words express so eloquently my feelings about how different things have been for me from the beginning of my journey until now. "At one time I was the darker sister. They send me to eat in the kitchen and company comes but I laughed and eat well and grow strong." These are the words written by Langston Hughes, who also said, "Tomorrow I will be at the table when company comes.

Nobody will dare say to me eat in the kitchen again besides, they'll see how beautiful I am and be ashamed I too am America. As for me at this moment of my life, I no longer sit in the kitchen. I am considered now the beautiful one. The people who once discriminated against me, now see me as an equal. Some I'm sure now feel ashamed." As Hughes meant by his words, I too feel the same way sometimes, especially being honored so frequently by folks who look like the same people who looked down on me and thought of me as only a domestic worker or field hand in my youth – But as it happens, people change as times change. Now I sign the autographs, and now I tell my story, and it is a good feeling and has been worth the wait. Again, God is good.

A point of reference: for the first time in history, Miss America, Miss USA, Miss Teen USA, and Miss Universe were all women of color recently. That was amazing for little girls of color to see, even if only for one year. Seeing someone who looks like them with those titles can only inspire them to dream more realistically. They say if you live long enough, you will see everything, but that's something (along with a person of color in the White House) that I thought I would never see. I guess folks thought they would never see black mathematicians in top-secret positions in the government at one time too, but we got started in late 1955, in all shades of brown. Sometimes change is painfully slow, but it will come in time, with faith and persistence.

When I think back to my first days at Dahlgren, I remember it being my first experience with integration – my first time sitting down and working with white co-workers. We were an experiment in a way, I suppose. President Dwight D. Eisenhower signed Executive Order 10590, establishing the President's Committee on Government Policy to enforce a nondiscrimination policy in Federal Government. So maybe that was all the incentive that Mr. Ralph Niemann needed to recruit black professionals to Dahlgren. Or maybe he had a vision that was invisible to the others. Like the vision I had of getting off that farm and doing something with my life that none of the others could see or imagine. I wondered how the white employees at Dahlgren would react since many of them had not worked or associated with black professionals before. I think so often of the other black employees, who like Ira and myself, were finally getting an opportunity to prove that they could perform as well as their white counterparts. We all became not only colleagues, but friends as well. It was like a family, and we knew we could lean on each other if we had to. Another husband and wife couple, Lottie and Harold, come to mind, so do Clara, Herman, Jesse, Orbie, Otis, Pearl, and Wendell. "Could we handle it" was the question that was most likely whispered behind closed doors and throughout the hallways of our building? Would we have the professionalism to handle the obvious distractions that we would encounter? We were well prepared for the doubters, though. For the most part, we were told what to expect from our amazing teachers and professors, who had taught, trained, and mentored us, as if we were their own.

Looking back, I would say we more than held our own in that environment. It is often said to surround yourself with the right people...people who inspire you, not people who will bring you down. That is how I would describe that first group of black professionals who always lifted each other up. This group, along with some others who followed, contributed greatly to the projects and research that made Dahlgren a key component to the success of the Navy, and to America.

In our minds, it was not only the patriotic thing to do, it was a matter of pride. We were a few bright minds, mostly from black colleges and very humble backgrounds, who were proving that we could accomplish anything if given an opportunity – just like Mr. Niemann had envisioned we would do when he came up with the not so popular idea to hire us back in the 1950s. It was important that we did not fail, so that other black scientists and mathematicians would be able to come behind us and contribute as well. After all those years of outstanding work and accomplishments, and the many personal challenges, I am starting to feel like I have come full circle. I always seemed to have some challenge before me. What do I do now?

I could write my life story, but who would believe it, right? Nevertheless, I decided that would be a good project, and hopefully, you are enjoying that decision right about now. One other thing I had always thought about doing was to work with a scholarship fund. The Dahlgren Heritage Museum is a small non-profit organization in our community dedicated to preserving, interpreting, displaying, and maintaining the artifacts that are the physical, intellectual, social, and cultural heritage of the U.S. Navy Base and community at Dahlgren. The Museum was interested in teaming up with Ira and me to establish a mathematics scholarship in our honor. One of the museum's objectives is to tell the stories of the community's many contributions to the Navy and accomplishments of its lifelong Dahlgren employees, such as ourselves. Ira for his work on Submarine-launched Ballistic Missiles programs and becoming one of the first black supervisors on the base; and me for my work, which contributed to the development of GPS. The museum was also aware of our continued work with elementary school students by enhancing their reading and mathematics skills through mentoring, and they felt we would be well suited to start a mathematics scholarship fund. As a recipient of a scholarship myself, I know how important it is for students to have the ability to afford higher education, especially for those pursuing mathematics and other STEM degrees.

As college costs continue to rise, they felt there was no time like the present to get started with the Ira and Gladys West Scholarship Fund. The project got off to a great start in 2019 as we hosted a scholarship dinner to help achieve the minimum endowment level. The event was attended by so many former colleagues, friends, and family, and included dignitaries from Naval Officers to U.S. Diplomats. From that one event and with donations that followed, we are just about there. Each year the scholarship fund will award at least one annual scholarship of $1000 to a graduating senior in King George County. The Dahlgren Heritage Museum believes in the hidden power of an education rich in math and science, and we are so grateful to the Museum for creating this scholarship in our honor. Priority will be given to high achieving and highly motivated students with a demonstrated financial need. It is a blessing to contribute to the scholarship fund, helping to provide college funds for young people who have the desire for an education but do not have the money. Ira and I know this all too well, as we were poor and had nothing as children. We believe there is a young "Ira or Gladys" somewhere out there just needing that extra financial support. There may be some young girl or boy out there who can help cure or immunize the dreaded global diseases that are an immense threat to society and to our world, now and even more in the future. What if there is a little girl with a twinkle in her eye, but with no money to further her education, who can come up with a solution to world hunger, or eradicate the senseless gun violence as we know all too well and experience every day in this nation? Nothing is impossible, and I know personally that those young people are among us. I walked in their shoes many decades ago. We must give them not only inspiration and motivation but provide them with the financial resources they need to gain the knowledge and skills to accomplish their dreams, to serve the next generation, and to be great. The inventors, visionaries, and the truly gifted are often from the least likely of backgrounds. Let's give them a chance to make a difference. There is no limit to what they can achieve.

This past Black History Month was so busy as it seemed everyone wanted to recognize me as a history maker and role model. I would like to thank Diversity in Action Magazine, HRT Radio in Los Angeles, and the Black Heritage Breakfast at Second Elam Baptist Church in New Kent, Virginia, for giving me a platform to share my story. The interviews were delightful, and Second Elam Baptist Church, your hospitality was warm and gracious, so don't be surprised if you see me again as a visitor one Sunday morning. I won't even comment on the delicious breakfast; you already know! I spoke at the YMCA in King George, to the Active Older Adult Luncheon recently for well over 20 minutes, and it made me feel grateful for the training and confidence I gained with Toastmistress International. I could never have done that in my early days at Dahlgren. How is that for professional development?

Other happenings recently included a Black History Month spotlight by AARP's social/digital campaign. This was significant since the $1500 honorarium received from AARP for my likeness went to our Scholarship Foundation. Additionally, I was presented with a Senate

Joint Resolution by the Virginia General Assembly for Black History Month. The resolution commended me for my 42-year career at Dahlgren, and for *"valuable contributions to the development of the GPS, and vital contributions to modern technology."* It was resolved by the Senate and concurred on by the House of Delegates. What a big honor with all those politicians applauding for me at the Virginia State Capital, where so much history had taken place since 1788. This time my eyes may have watered a bit, but it was because I was thinking, "Look at me Ma Macy. I wonder what ole Thomas Jefferson is thinking right about now."

Another of my favorites recently was receiving an honorary membership into the Virginia Association of Surveyors (VAS). Gary Faulhaber, President of the association, noted in an article that followed, "Today, by far, was one of the greatest moments of my Presidency. I was totally in awe of her humility and kindness." When I told him of my 16-year-old grandson, David, Jr's interest in becoming a surveyor, he commented on how cool that would be for him to become a surveyor and a future member of VAS. He even invited him to apply for a scholarship from the organization's Education Trust. That's important to know that all the hard work and challenges I met and persevered through the right way, will mean something to my children and their children. Dave Doyle (Honorary Member of VAS, and former Chief Geodetic Surveyor of the National Geodetic Survey) commented, "Meeting Dr. West has to be one of the most memorable events in my career. Her pioneering activities and significant achievements in geodesy, accomplished in the face of so many challenges, combined with her humility, love of family and country should be an inspiration to all of us." Words like that are directly attributable to my upbringing. I was Ma Macy's child for sure, and I give her and God all the credit. Some people say all this recognition is coming too late, but I'm still here on this not so round earth, so I believe that good things come to those who wait, and it's just my time.

I also believe it's never too late for change and for people to acknowledge the wrongs of the past and do their best to never let the past resurface. It's hard for those who did the perpetrating to apologize and do what is right to make amends. It is just as difficult for those who suffered from the mistreatment to accept those apologies. It is my feeling that we must forgive, but demand reparations and never forget the actions of the past. For it is the responsibility of all of us to make certain that the atrocities of slavery and segregation never appear again, and discrimination for any reason be eliminated from our society. That is something we all must strive for through our example, values, and day to day life choices, no matter your race, religion, or culture. We may look different, speak differently, dress differently, but we are all one race – the "human race." Thus, before you analyze the world's problems regarding racism, sexism, or any other form of discrimination, take a good look at yourself. There may be something that you can do better, as a parent, a teacher, a student, and a co-worker, just like Ira and I did with my doctoral classmate. He was a different man after we got to know one another. It's all about respecting and treating others as you want them to treat you. We must stand up for equality and justice for all of us. Only then will we be a truly great America.

I still think of all those young men who were training to go overseas and fight for our country at the start of World War II. I remember how I looked on in amazement at their faces while on my way to our

195

segregated schoolhouse on Butterwood Road. That picture of those soldiers from Fort Lee on bivouac in the fields of Dinwiddie County as they prepared to protect this nation is still embedded in my memory. They were fighting for all of us, no matter what our color. Somehow the white boys parted with Jim Crow for a minute and took on Uncle Sam as their man. Even if only for that provisional moment, they were willing to fight for all of us. Likewise, the "colored" boys were not colored anymore, as they volunteered in high numbers, and were willing to die for our country. We were all Americans, one team, one race. That's when I first recognized what patriotism is all about, and that word, as difficult as it was to swallow many times in my life, has always been entrenched in my mind, filling my heart with pride, and inspiring me to commit myself to make things better in this world through my work, my character, my spirituality, and my values.

I recall reading *A Dream Deferred* by Langston Hughes while I was an undergraduate student at Virginia State. Hughes wrote, "Hold fast to your dreams, for if dreams die, life is a broken-winged bird that cannot fly. What happens to a dream deferred? Does it dry up like a raisin in the sun?" Reading those words as a young woman helped me realize how important it was to pursue my dreams and my purpose. I would be that same little girl continuing to work in the tobacco fields the rest of my life as the others had done before me, without my dreams. Those dreams were filled with the hopes and aspirations that no one could take away from me if I believed in them and made them my reality. I stepped into my dream, and it was who I had become.

It can happen to any of you as well. Our country and the world are counting on you. What will you do with your dreams? Are you willing to go beyond society's normal expectations of you? For all the little girls and young women out there – The world needs more scientists, physicists, engineers, mathematicians, computer technologists, medical doctors, researchers and lawmakers, and there is no reason why they can't be women. It's all right to think and dream of that road less traveled that may lead you to an imaginative, exciting career and future. I accomplished some things in my life that no one else would have imagined for a little black girl who grew up on a small farm during The Great Depression, in segregated Dinwiddie County, Virginia, and I am still being honored, thanked and commended for that work today. It's all so overwhelming and hard to believe, and to think – It began with a dream.

A dream and a vision of a road that would take me on this incredible journey, navigating my way so differently from my predecessors, because of that dream. The work ethic and commitment were the same as theirs in the past, but it was a different time, and the amazing people I encountered along the way were life-changers who gave me the motivation and opportunity to seek a different way of life. My thoughts that were unimaginable to others were a blessing to me, and I believed in them. My optimistic adventures led me down a road rarely taken in those times, with no map or direction, but with something much more guiding and positioning. That road was paved with faith, hope, love, commitment, and a desire to be the best. That was the set of values I lived by, and that I prayed would lead me more precisely to my dream of happiness – and it did. Imagine that – then imagine it for yourself.

I was the Grand Marshal at the 2018 Virginia State University Homecoming Parade with Dr. Abdullah in background.

Virginia State University President Abdullah was present, along with 2018-19 NBCA Hall of Fame Queen, Brittany Dorsey, for my induction into the National Black College Alumni Hall of Fame in Atlanta, Georgia.

With General Thompson at my induction into the Air Force Missile and Space Pioneers Hall of Fame.

Speaking to the audience at the Hall of Fame induction at the Pentagon.

Lt. Colonel Lacresha Griffin Merkle, USAF, thanked me for opening doors for women like her.

The Air Force Space and Missile Pioneers HOF Ceremony souvenir program.

The Fulton Bank and Fahrenheit Advisors Black History Month tribute to me. Artist Jerome Jones and his son, Jeromyah surprised me with a lovely portrait.

I was honored by my home county at the Dinwiddie County Government Center. VSU alumnus Charmica Epps was on hand.

VSU President, Dr. Abdullah, after he spoke on my behalf at the Dinwiddie County Event.

Karla Redditte (KarlaNBC12) the Mistress of Ceremony
with me at the Dominion Virginia Event after the Dominion
Virginia Awards Ceremony.

Carolyn and her husband Barry and Andre and his wife Lia with Ira and me.

We were mentoring children at a speaking engagement
in Fort Washington, Maryland. This is one of our passions.

We were grand marshals at the King George parade.

GPS display at our Scholarship Fundraiser Dinner.

Dr. Gladys B. West

ACKNOWLEDGMENTS

Above and beyond all, God has always kept me a member and grounded in the Rocky Branch Baptist Church in Sutherland, Virginia where I was raised. Thank you for always welcoming me home, lifting me up, expressing love, and concern and well wishes. God is good!

I could not have written this book if it were not for my mother, Macy Pearl Brown, who believed in me, uplifted me, and inspired me during her life. She taught me so much and I will always hold her close to my heart.

Who knew that a simple phone call from the daughter of an old friend would develop into a deep connection and the chance to have my story written. Dorcas Watson, daughter of the late Orbie Jones who was the fifth black professional hired at Dahlgren, and her friend, Marvin Jackson, who along with a few family members and friends, listened to my story and understood my dream. Marvin magically turned my dreams into this beautifully written story about my life. Our families have connected and working almost two years with them has been such an enjoyable experience. I thank you both, from the bottom of my heart, for believing in my story, making me proud of my accomplishments and for assisting me in writing my memoirs to help encourage others to dream.

To my husband, Ira V. West, I have endless gratitude for your unconditional love and encouragement through all my endeavors. You have been by my side continuously, listening to my vision, and guiding me to bring it to actuality, and carefully and patiently reading each chapter to ensure that the integrity of my story was intact. I am elated that my story is published and there is no greater joy than to share this journey with you beside me!

My only daughter, Carolyn Oglesby, I thank you for always being there offering encouragement, guiding the many pieces together, and using her expertise to find what was most needed. Thank you to her husband Barry for patiently standing by her side and supporting me. Thanks for always keeping us on point and having plans made for a scrumptious meal.

My son, David West, with his Geographic Information System expertise, as he made trips to Dinwiddie county to obtain maps that showed key places of interest, such as Butterwood Elementary School, Dinwiddie Training High School, and the main Dinwiddie County Government Buildings. Thank you and your family for a job well done.

My son, Michael West, I thank you for your genuine concern for my safety and well-being. The support from your family is appreciated.

My oldest grandchild, Andre Jones with his creative vision, was excited about designing a cover and selecting the photography that showed all my strong points and his vision of me. You make me proud. I love the cover and I thank you and Lia for always making time for me.

A special note of thanks to Lt. General Stayce D. Harris, USAF (Retired) who attended my induction into the Air Force Space and Missile Pioneers Hall of Fame ceremony. Her words gave me such clarity and confidence that others need to hear my story. Thank you for writing the foreword to my book. Your words inspire and give hope to others.

Special thanks to Erica Young for her editorial expertise. I appreciate your attention to detail and your contributions toward making this book become a reality. You made our job easier and I thank you for being there for us.

My dreams are rooted in the Dinwiddie County schools. Many thanks to my elementary and high school teachers who prepared me academically and prepared me for life, especially for the rough times they knew would come. They showed love, concern for my needs, kept me safe and most importantly, they believed in me.

A huge heartfelt thank you to Dr. Louise Hunter, a mathematics professor at VSC, who saw potential in me and knew that she could depend on me. Going to college with adequate funding was one of my biggest challenges. By hiring me to care for her daughter during the last three years of college, she resolved my funding concerns, and she gave me the boost to continue my dreams, to be the best me, to help others and to always be committed.

I am indebted to Virginia State College (one of the Historically Black Colleges and Universities), that provided the strong academic curriculum in mathematics that is the basis for my career; and that gave me strong role models, who stood on firm foundations, who had visions, and who had a purpose for their lives. This was inspirational for me and another step on the path of my dreams.

A special thank you to Ralph Niemann, Head of the Computation and Analysis Department, who hired me as one of the first minorities at the Naval Proving Ground, Dahlgren, Virginia. Thanks for believing in me, giving me training, and for the opportunity to contribute to the needs of the country. I am also grateful for the many others who helped me to be the best that I could be during my career at Dahlgren.

The Alpha Kappa Alpha Sorority has been a part of my life since 1950. Thank you for being an organization of educated, strong, intelligent women who are willing to serve their community and be their best. Thank you for being a stabilizing force in my life and keeping me focused on looking upward and outward.

My utmost appreciation and gratitude for all the individuals and organizations who have humbled me by honoring my work, achievements, and accomplishments, and who continue to share my story. I have met hundreds of people through these events and continue to be inspired by all whom I meet.

I am blessed and grateful to have a loving, caring extended family and friends who have touched my life and made an impact in many ways along my journey. I would not be here today without each of you. I thank you all!

The Ira and Gladys West Scholarship Fund was created in our honor by the Dahlgren Heritage Museum. They will award at least one annual scholarship of $1,000 to a graduating high school senior in King George County. With this scholarship, they hope to support students pursuing a degree in mathematics or science. Priority will be given to high achieving and highly motivated students with demonstrated financial need. You may donate to the scholarship fund or to get information by contacting the foundation below:

The Community Foundation
P.O. Box 208
Fredericksburg, Virginia 22404.0208
(540) 373-9292
Or visit us on Facebook at drgladysbwest

ABOUT THE AUTHOR

Born in Dinwiddie County, Virginia, Dr. Gladys B. West earned a tuition scholarship to Virginia State College (now University), She has B.S and M.S. degrees in Mathematics from Virginia State. She was hired as a mathematician in 1956 at what is now the Dahlgren Surface Naval Warfare Center, She played an integral role in the development of the Global Positioning System (GPS), and retired after 42 years of service. She has a master's degree in Public Administration from Oklahoma University and a Ph.D. in Public Administration from Virginia Tech. She was inducted into the Air Force Missile and Space Pioneers Hall of Fame and the National Black College Alumni Hall of Fame. She and her husband Ira West have been married 63 years. They have three adult children, seven grandchildren and two great grandchildren.

Made in the USA
Coppell, TX
06 November 2022

85891050R00132